Purpose Of Life

The Ripple Effect of Inner Peace

Arun Tiwari
celebrated co-author of *Wings of Fire*

Sakāl
Publications

Sakāl
Publications

PURPOSE OF LIFE

Sakal Media Pvt. Ltd.
595, Budhwar Peth,
Pune–411002, India
www.sakalmediagroup.com
sakalpublications.com
sakalprakashan@esakal.com

First Edition: October, 2025

ISBN: 978-93-49487-80-2

Cover Design: Rohit K.
Typesetting: MAP Systems, Bengaluru

Printed in India by Sakal Media Pvt. Ltd.

Contents

Introduction

There are hours when the ordinary rhythm of life falters—the kettle cools upon the stove, the clock ticks with unfamiliar insistence, and the mind, like a bird startled from its branch, lifts into the vastness of the sky. In such moments, a question steals upon us, unbidden yet insistent: *Why am I here?* It is not a question of bread or shelter, not a matter of gain or loss, but of essence, of being. And once uttered, it lingers, echoing in the caverns of the self.

English writer Virginia Woolf (1882–1941) once wrote, "*Arrange whatever pieces come your way.*" And yet, how does one arrange them—the fragments of thought, the broken mosaics of desire, the scattered beads of days—without first sensing the thread that binds them? That thread is the purpose. Without it, the pieces remain a restless clutter, shimmering perhaps, but without song.

Purpose does not dictate the shape in advance; it whispers direction, like a current beneath the surface, guiding fragments into a pattern where each shard finds its light. To live without purpose is to shuffle endlessly, moving pieces from here to there in a ceaseless noise of activity. To live with purpose is to weave, to discover that even what seemed broken or misplaced has a place in the design. It is the invisible thread that turns fragments into form, randomness into rhythm, days into meaning.

This book is about that pause, that silence between heartbeat and breath, where the pulse of existence feels both fragile and eternal.

To speak of the purpose of life is not to hand down a doctrine, but to enter into conversation with one's own soul, with the whisper of the body, with the unseen order of things. It is to linger in the stillness where words dissolve and meanings emerge, to attend to that subtle place where fear softens into wonder and doubt gives way to listening. Purpose is not imposed from without, like a rule carved into stone; it unfolds from within, like a flower turning toward the sun.

In that unfolding, silence becomes a teacher, showing us that the most profound truths arrive not as proclamations but as intimations—faint at first, like the hush before dawn, yet steady, insistent, shaping the contours of our days. This beginning, then, is not a command but an invitation: to lean closer, to listen deeper, to let the hidden rhythm of existence draw us into dialogue with life itself.

There are two parts – Principles and Practices. What is given and what we take. The background and the forefront, the eternal and the ephemeral, the universal and the personal, the sky and the cloud, the Sun and the lamp...

In Principles, we touch the threads that run beneath the fabric: the search for meaning in existence, the restless dance of the mind, the whirlpool of shallow thought that drags us down, the longed-for unity of mind and body, and the ancient, ever-receding idea of God. As Gurudev Rabindranath Tagore (1861-1941) reminds us, *"Faith is the bird that feels the light and sings when the dawn is still dark."* These principles are our first glimmers of light, before the day has yet begun.

The second part turns towards Practices. For thought, if left alone, grows brittle. It must spill into life, into gesture, into breath. We shall look upon the world and see God shimmering in the phenomenon, feel Him in the secret chamber of the heart, walk through the mind as though it were a portal opening into unseen vistas, and at last, stand before that ultimate experience where the self dissolves into something greater.

To live with this awareness is to live with gentleness toward oneself, with trust in what cannot yet be named. The invitation here is not to force clarity but to dwell in mystery, to hold the questions tenderly until they flower into answers of their own accord. In this way, the most common moments—an unnoticed breeze, a smile exchanged, a grief endured—become thresholds, openings through which the soul's hidden spring slowly, inevitably, arrives.

These pages are not a map but a mirror. They do not prescribe a road; they reflect the many roads already beneath your feet. You may wander them in order or in chance, as life itself allows. For the search for purpose is not linear—it spirals, it drifts, it circles back upon itself until, one day, the familiar is seen as if for the first time, and the hidden meaning shines through. To read, then, is not to be led but to be reminded: that every pause, every detour, every return carries its own quiet necessity.

The purpose of life—perhaps it is not to be sought far away, in unreachable heavens, but awakened within, quietly, as dawn awakens a sleeping village, unhurried yet unstoppable. In that awakening, existence ceases to be merely endured; it becomes luminous, trembling with significance, like a lamp lit from within. And so, dear reader, let us begin—not with certainty, but with openness; not with answers, but with the courage to dwell in questions. For it is in the spaces between them, in the hush before clarity, that life's true purpose flickers into view and, if you are attentive, may just catch fire in your own heart.

Arun Tiwari

Hyderabad
September 2025

Part I: Principles

In today's fast-paced, interconnected environment, cultivating a purposeful life requires intentionality and deeper reflection. Key principles to guide this journey include seeking meaning in existence, engaging the mind with real work, avoiding a downward spiral of shallow thinking, uniting the mind and body, and viewing the divine as a sustaining and compassionate presence. By applying these principles, individuals can discover a deeper purpose beyond fleeting pleasures or superficial pursuits. In the interconnected modern world, a purposeful life rooted in meaning, mindful engagement, depth, unity, and spiritual trust leads to a more fulfilling, resilient, and compassionate existence.

1

Seeking Meaning in Existence

"Man is condemned to be free, because once thrown into the world, he is responsible for everything he does. It is up to you to give [life] a meaning."

—Jean-Paul Sartre
French philosopher (1905 –1980)
1964 Nobel Prize in Literature

1. Exploration of Purpose

In the vast expanse of the universe, humanity has always grappled with one profound question: What is the purpose of a human life? For millennia, philosophers, spiritual leaders, scientists, and ordinary people alike have pondered this fundamental inquiry. While answers abound and perspectives differ across cultures and eras, the simplest terms often resonate most deeply. Stripped of complexity, the purpose of human life can be summed up in a single phrase: to live, to connect, and to find meaning.

Living, in its most basic sense, is the act of existing—to breathe, to move, to experience. Every living being, from the smallest microbe to the most enormous whale, shares this fundamental drive. For humans, life is an intricate tapestry woven from moments both ordinary and extraordinary. To live is to embrace the full spectrum of human experience: joy and sorrow, success and failure, hope and despair.

In a broader sense, living can also be seen as the journey of navigating through time, making choices, and experiencing the consequences of those choices. It is a dynamic process that varies significantly across different forms of life, from simple organisms to complex beings like humans, who often seek meaning, purpose, and fulfilment in their existence.

So, living is not just about survival. It is about growth—learning new things, overcoming challenges, and adapting to change. It is about exploration, curiosity, and wonder. As children, we explore our surroundings with insatiable curiosity, and as adults, we continue to seek new experiences, relationships, and understandings. In living, we fulfil our biological imperative, but we also create space for something greater: awareness and appreciation of our existence.

2. Network of Human Connections

Our lives are deeply intertwined with the relationships we build, the communities we belong to, and the broader social structures we navigate. We rely on others for survival, emotional support, and personal growth. From family and friends to colleagues and strangers, our lives are shaped by the connections we form. These relationships create a web of interdependence, where the actions of one person can ripple through the network, affecting others.

2.1 Existentialism

While existentialists like Jean-Paul Sartre emphasise individual freedom and responsibility, they also acknowledge that relationships play a crucial role in shaping our existence. Our connections with others can both constrain and enrich our liberty. Russian novelist Fyodor Dostoevsky (1821–1881) wrote, "Above all, don't lie to yourself. The man who lies to himself and listens to his lie comes to a point that he cannot distinguish the truth within him, or around him." Humans are not born with a predetermined purpose or essence. Instead, we first exist, and then we must define ourselves through our choices, actions, and the experiences that follow. In other words, we create our meaning in an otherwise indifferent or absurd universe.

2.2 Ubuntu Philosophy

In African philosophy, the concept of Ubuntu ("I am because we are") highlights the interconnectedness of humanity. It suggests that our society is defined through our relationships with others. Nelson Mandela (1918–2013) explained that Ubuntu is not about rejecting personal success, but about ensuring that your success benefits the broader community. He said, "Ubuntu does not mean that people should not enrich themselves. The question is: Are you going to do so to enable the community around you to improve?" Our humanity is deeply tied to the humanity of others. It is a reminder that we cannot exist in isolation—our identities, well-being, and purpose are shaped by our connections with the community. Ubuntu calls us to recognise our interconnectedness and to act with compassion, solidarity, and care for one another.

2.3 Systems Theory

From a sociological perspective, life can be viewed as a complex system in which individuals are nodes within a larger network. Changes in one part of the network can affect the entire system, illustrating the interdependence of human life. French author Victor Hugo (1802–1885) highlights the tension between individual ambition and the collective nature of society, suggesting that societal systems often enforce conformity. He writes, "Society is a republic. When an individual tries to lift themselves above others, they are dragged down by the mass, either by ridicule or slander."
According to American author Edward Abbey (1927–1989), "Society is like a stew. If you don't stir it up every once in a while, the scum rises to the top." As a system, society requires constant engagement and critique to prevent stagnation or the dominance of harmful elements. Society is indeed a machine which runs on the gears of cooperation, but often grinds individuals in the process. There is always an ongoing tension between the system's need for order and the individual's desire for freedom.

3. Meaning is the Compass

Just as a compass provides direction, meaning gives life a sense of purpose. It helps us navigate through challenges, make decisions, and prioritise what truly matters. Without meaning, life can feel aimless or adrift. When we have a clear sense of meaning, we are better equipped to face adversity. Meaning acts as an anchor, helping us stay grounded during life's storms. It provides a reason to keep going, even when the path is difficult. Viktor Frankl (1905–1997), in his book *Man's Search for Meaning*, argues that the primary drive in human life is not pleasure or power, but rather the search for meaning. Frankl, a Holocaust survivor, observed that those who found meaning, even in the most horrific circumstances, were more resilient and able to endure suffering.

Meaning can be deeply personal—found in relationships, passions, or personal goals—but it can also be collective, derived from contributing to something larger than ourselves, such as a community, society, or a cause. Both forms of meaning are essential for a fulfilling life. When meaning is absent, life can feel empty or meaningless, leading to existential crises. This is often referred to as the existential vacuum, a state in which individuals experience a profound sense of emptiness or a lack of purpose. In today's fast-paced and often fragmented world, finding meaning can be a challenge. The rise of individualism, consumerism, and technological distractions can sometimes obscure more profound questions of purpose. Yet, the search for meaning remains a fundamental human endeavour.

Our sense of meaning is closely tied to our identity. What we find meaningful often reflects our values, beliefs, and experiences. It shapes who we are and how we see ourselves in the world. Conversely, the things we find meaningful often reinforce our identity. When we engage in activities or relationships that align with our sense of self, we feel more authentic and fulfilled. This creates a positive feedback loop where meaning strengthens identity, and identity deepens our understanding of meaning. When our identity is disrupted through significant life changes, trauma, or existential questioning, our sense of meaning can also be thrown into crisis. This is often referred to as an identity crisis, where individuals struggle to find purpose or direction because their sense of self is in a state of flux.

4. Life Narratives

We live by the stories we tell ourselves and others about our lives. These narratives play a crucial role in shaping our identity. They help us answer the question, "Who am I?" by providing a sense of continuity and coherence across different stages of life. Through life narratives, we interpret our experiences and assign meaning to them. Our life narratives help us create a sense of continuity and coherence, linking our past, present, and future. This process helps us understand ourselves better and make sense of our emotions, motivations, and actions.

4.1 The Role of Memory

Memory plays a crucial role in shaping our life narratives. However, memory is not a perfect record of events; it is selective and often reconstructed. We tend to remember events that fit into our existing narratives and forget or reinterpret those that do not. This means our life narratives are constantly evolving as we reinterpret our past. Like any good story, life narratives have plots and themes. The plot is the sequence of events, while the theme is the underlying message or moral of the story. For example, someone might see their life as a journey of self-discovery (theme) with key turning points (plot) that led to personal growth. Colombian writer Gabriel García Márquez (1927–2014), who won the 1982 Nobel Prize in Literature, writes, "Life is not what one lived, but what one remembers and how one remembers it to recount it."

4.2 The Role of Others in Shaping Our Narratives

Our life narratives are not created in isolation; the people around us shape them. Family, friends, and society have a considerable influence on the stories we tell about ourselves. For example, a parent's expectations or societal norms can shape how we see our achievements and failures. As we age, our life narratives often shift towards a focus on legacy—what we will leave behind for future generations. This can involve reflecting on our accomplishments, the impact we have had on others, and the values we want to pass on. The people who are closest to us—those who love, challenge, and inspire us—play a crucial role in shaping the stories we tell about ourselves. There is an anonymous quote saying, "The stories we tell about ourselves are co-authored by the people who love us, challenge us, and inspire us." Not only are we the stories we tell ourselves, but we are also the stories others refuse to let us forget.

4.3 The Universality of Life Narratives

While the content of our life narratives is unique to each individual, the act of creating narratives is a universal experience. Across cultures and throughout history, humans have used stories to make sense of their lives and their place in the world. While life narratives can be empowering, they can also be limiting. Stories that focus on failure, victimhood, or inadequacy can trap us in a cycle of self-doubt and inaction. Recognising and challenging these narratives is crucial for mental health and well-being. There is a universal need to share our stories, suggesting that storytelling is essential to human well-being. According to American writer and civil rights activist Maya Angelou (1928–2014), "There is no greater agony than bearing an untold story inside you."

5. Need to be Loved

If we distil the purpose of human life to its purest essence—beyond living and connecting—it often comes down to love. The need to be loved is a profound and universal human experience that drives much of our behaviour, relationships, and emotional well-being. The need to be loved shapes and influences our relationships, emotions, and overall well-being.

5.1 Biological and Evolutionary Basis

From an evolutionary perspective, love and connection are essential for survival. Early humans relied on social bonds for protection, cooperation, and the care and raising of their offspring. The need to be loved is deeply ingrained in our biology, as it promotes attachment and bonding, which are crucial for survival and reproduction. Brazilian author Paulo Coelho (b. 1947) defines love as an evolutionary force. He writes, "Love is not to be found in someone else, but in ourselves; we simply awaken it. But to do that, we need the other person." While relationships are essential, the foundation of love begins with self-awareness and self-acceptance. By understanding this, we can approach love with a sense of wholeness and authenticity.

5.2 Emotional Well-Being

Love and acceptance are fundamental to our emotional health. Feeling loved contributes to a sense of security, self-worth, and happiness. Conversely, a lack of love or rejection can lead to feelings of loneliness, anxiety, and depression. Love provides emotional support, helping us navigate life's challenges with greater resilience. Whether it is romantic love, familial love, or friendship, these connections fulfil our need for belonging and community. Being loved helps us feel understood, valued, and connected to others, which is essential for a fulfilling life. Love has the power to heal emotional wounds and foster personal growth. When we feel loved, we are more likely to open up, trust others, and work through difficulties. Love can provide the emotional safety net needed to explore our vulnerabilities and become our best selves.

5.3 Self-Esteem and Identity

Being loved by others often reinforces our sense of self-worth and identity. When we feel loved, we are more likely to see ourselves in a positive light and feel confident in our abilities. Love can validate our existence and give us a sense of purpose. The desire to be loved can drive many of our actions and decisions. We may go out of our way to help others, pursue relationships, or engage in activities that make us feel valued and appreciated. This need can motivate us to build and maintain healthy relationships, which are essential for personal growth and happiness.

5.4 The Paradox of Love

While the need to be loved is powerful, it can also lead to challenges. The fear of not being loved or of losing love can cause anxiety, insecurity, and even unhealthy behaviours. It is essential to strike a balance between the desire for love, self-love, and independence, ensuring that our need for external validation does not overshadow our internal sense of worth. Love is both liberating and overwhelming, impossible to control or comprehend fully. According to Paulo Coelho, love is both liberating and overwhelming, and it is impossible to fully control or comprehend. He writes, "Love is an untamed force. When we try to control it, it destroys us. When we try to imprison it, it enslaves us. When we try to understand it, it leaves us feeling lost and confused."

While the pursuit of love can be complex and sometimes challenging, it remains a central part of the human experience, offering profound meaning and fulfilment in life. Love is a terrific and perhaps the only force capable of turning an ordinary moment into an extraordinary memory.

6. Purpose in Everyday Life

While grand philosophies may seek to answer the question on a cosmic scale, the purpose of life is often found in daily routines and simple acts. By embracing the ordinary, practising mindfulness, and finding joy in the little things, we can uncover a deep sense of meaning and fulfilment in our everyday lives. After all, it is the small moments that, when woven together, create the tapestry of a life well-lived.

Daily routines—whether it is making tea, tending a plant, attending to a pet, or cooking a meal—ground us, providing a sense of stability and continuity. They remind us that life is not just about significant achievements, but also about the quiet, consistent moments that shape our days.

Simple acts of kindness, like holding the door for someone, sharing a smile, or listening to a friend, can create profound connections. These moments remind us that the essence of life is often found in how we treat others and the small ways we make the world a better place.

Every day, waking up with gratitude, helping a neighbour in need, learning something new, creating art, music, or stories, spending time with loved ones, caring for the environment, offering forgiveness and understanding, building a legacy for future generations—such little virtuous everyday moments, strung together, create a life of meaning and fulfilment.

7. The Role of Individual Choice

Each person shapes their purpose through choices, values, and aspirations. Some may dedicate their lives to a cause, while others dedicate themselves to family or discovery. Some seek adventure, while others cherish stability. The diversity of human purpose is as vast as humanity itself. What matters is the authenticity of one's path and the intention behind each step. Our choices become the guiding force that shapes our purpose and helps us navigate life's journey with clarity and intention. By exercising our autonomy, defining our values, and making intentional decisions, we can craft a life that feels meaningful and fulfilling. While we may not always control our circumstances, we always have the power to choose our attitude, actions, and responses.

7.1 Personal Agency and Autonomy

One of the most powerful aspects of being human is the ability to make choices. Whether it is choosing a career, forming relationships, or pursuing passions, our decisions shape the direction of our lives. This autonomy allows us to craft a life that aligns with our values and aspirations. Recognising that we are the architects of our own lives can be both empowering and daunting, but it is a crucial step in finding purpose. When we make choices based on our true selves rather than external expectations, we live more authentically.

This authenticity is key to finding a sense of purpose and fulfilment. Albert Einstein (1879–1955) writes, "The one who follows the crowd will usually go no further than the crowd. The one who walks alone is likely to find himself in places no one has ever been before." Authenticity often requires going against the grain and forging one's path. Authenticity is not about perfection or fitting into a mould—it is about embracing your true self, flaws and all. It means living your own life, not someone else's version of it. According to the modern-age icon Steve Jobs (1955–2011), "Your time is limited, so don't waste it living someone else's life."

7.2 The Role of Intention

Purpose is often found when we live with intention. By making deliberate choices about how we spend our time and energy, we can create a life that feels meaningful and fulfilling. This might involve setting goals, practising mindfulness, or cultivating gratitude. When our actions align with our intentions, we experience a sense of coherence and purpose. This alignment is a powerful way to ensure that our choices are contributing to a life that feels purposeful.

Intention is more than just a thought or desire—it is a focused force that directs your energy and actions towards a specific outcome. These quotes remind us that intention is the starting point for creating meaningful change in our lives. Whether it is achieving goals, shaping habits, or transforming your reality, intention is the driving force that turns possibility into actuality. By setting clear, purposeful intentions, you can harness this power to create the life you envision.

Intention, when aligned with purpose, attracts the necessary support from the universe. Paulo Coelho writes, "When you want something, all the universe conspires in helping you to achieve it."

7.3 The Interplay Between Choice and Circumstance

While individual choice is powerful, it is essential to acknowledge that we do not always have control over our circumstances. However, even within constraints, we can choose our attitude and response. This ability to choose our perspective can be a source of great strength and purpose. By remaining open to change and willing to adapt our choices, we can continue to find meaning and fulfilment, even as our circumstances shift.

The choices we make today shape the legacy we leave behind. By living intentionally and making choices that align with our values, we can create a lasting impact that extends beyond our lifetimes. British writer C.S. Lewis (1898–1963) writes, "You can't go back and change the beginning, but you can start where you are and change the ending." While we cannot change our past circumstances, we can choose to shape a different future. Circumstances may shape the path, but it is our choices that determine the destination.

Challenges and growth are indeed hallmarks of life, shaping who we are and propelling us forward. Life is not without suffering, uncertainty, or loss. Yet, these challenges often become crucibles for growth and deeper purpose. Many people discover their true purpose and passions through the trials they face. Challenges usually lead to moments of clarity, where we reassess our priorities and align our actions with our deeper values.

8. Summary

In the simplest terms, the purpose of a human life is to live fully, connect deeply, and seek meaning, most often through love. Whether through relationships, achievements, creativity, or kindness, each person has the opportunity to make their life purposeful in their unique way. While definitive answers may elude us, the ongoing search for purpose is itself a vital part of being human. In the end, perhaps life's greatest purpose is to experience it—to cherish each moment, learn from each challenge, and share our journey with others.

2

Engaging the Mind

"The mind is its own place, and in itself
can make a heaven of hell, a hell of heaven."

— John Milton
English poet (1608 –1674)

1. The Finest Art of Living

To live is a simple act, but to live fully—engaging the mind in all its capacity—is the finest art of all. In a world overflowing with distractions and noise, cultivating an engaged, thoughtful mind stands as both a discipline and a reward. This document explores why engaging the mind is more than a mere pastime; it is the essence of a life well-lived, a daily practice that transforms existence from the mundane to the wondrous. The mind has the power to shape our perception of reality. Regardless of external circumstances, the mind can transform even the most difficult situations (hell) into something positive (heaven), or vice versa.

To engage the mind is to live with intention and awareness. It is to approach each day not as a series of tasks to complete, but as a canvas for curiosity, reflection, and growth. When we speak of "the art of living," we summon images of beauty, grace, and mastery. But unlike painting or music, the art of living is an internal process, one painted in the hues of thought, emotion, and understanding. The act of stimulating and challenging the intellect is one of the most fulfilling and meaningful aspects of life.

Mental engagement—whether through learning, creativity, problem-solving, or deep thought—is not just a pastime but a cornerstone of a rich and purposeful existence. When a person is not actively engaged in productive or meaningful activities, they are more likely to fall into negative behaviours, temptations, or harmful thoughts. It emphasises the importance of keeping the mind occupied with constructive pursuits to avoid falling into trouble or making poor decisions.

The mind can interpret and redefine reality based on its perspective. An idle mind can lead to overthinking, anxiety, or dwelling on negative emotions. Staying busy with positive activities helps maintain mental well-being. When people are unoccupied, they may be more susceptible to engaging in unhealthy or destructive behaviours, such as substance abuse, gossip, or other vices. Keeping the mind engaged reduces the likelihood of such temptations.

An active mind is more likely to seek out opportunities for learning, creativity, and self-improvement. Idleness, on the other hand, can lead to stagnation and the waste of potential. Having a routine or purpose helps people stay focused and disciplined. Without structure, it is easier to lose direction and fall into bad habits. In many religious or philosophical contexts, idleness is seen as a gateway to moral failings or sin. Staying engaged in virtuous activities is often encouraged to maintain spiritual and ethical integrity.

2. Awareness as the Foundation

At the core of engaging the mind lies awareness—the ability to observe oneself and the world with clarity. Awareness is not a passive state; it is an active, vigilant state that welcomes each moment with openness. It allows us to pause before reacting, to choose our responses, and to find meaning even in the most minor details of daily life. By being fully present and conscious of our thoughts, actions, and intentions, we can align ourselves with virtuous principles and make choices that reflect our highest values.

2.1 Self-Awareness

Awareness begins with understanding oneself—our thoughts, emotions, motivations, and biases. This self-knowledge allows us to recognise when we are acting out of alignment with our values and make conscious corrections. "Know thyself" is an Ancient Greek maxim inscribed at the Temple of Apollo at Delphi. It was a central idea in the teachings of Socrates (470–399 BCE) and other philosophers, who believed that self-knowledge is the foundation for wisdom and virtue.

2.2 Mindfulness

Mindfulness means maintaining a moment-by-moment awareness of our thoughts, feelings, bodily sensations, and surrounding environment through a gentle, nurturing lens. Living in this conscious way requires being present in the moment. Mindfulness enables us to observe our actions and reactions without judgment, allowing us to respond thoughtfully rather than react impulsively. Vietnamese Buddhist monk Thich Nhat Hanh (1926–2022) says, "The present moment is the only moment available to us, and it is the door to all moments." Every past and future moment is essentially a "now," a present experience. By focusing on the present, we can appreciate the fullness of time and avoid getting lost in thoughts of the past or future.

2.3 Breaking Unconscious Patterns

Many of our habits and behaviours are driven by unconscious conditioning, which operates outside of conscious awareness, leading to automatic responses and implicit learning. For example, we may develop a preference for a specific type of food without knowing why, or feel anxious in an environment without consciously recalling a past adverse event. Phobias can develop through unconscious conditioning, where a traumatic or damaging experience with a particular object or situation leads to an irrational fear. Awareness helps us break free from negative patterns and replace them with virtuous ones. Canadian–American psychotherapist Nathaniel Branden (1930–2014) writes, "The first step toward change is awareness. The second step is acceptance." American poet Emily Dickinson (1830–1886) said, "Forever is composed of nows."

2.4 Serenity Prayer

The Serenity Prayer is often attributed to American theologian Reinhold Niebuhr (1892 –1971), who wrote it in the 1930s.

> "God, grant me the serenity to accept the things I cannot change,
> Courage to change the things I can,
> And wisdom to know the difference."

It is often used in therapy and mindfulness practices to help people manage stress, anxiety, and feelings of helplessness. It encourages acceptance and proactive problem-solving, serving as a reminder to focus on what we can influence and let go of what we cannot. It is a cornerstone of the Alcoholics Anonymous (AA) programme, helping individuals focus on what they can control (their addictive behaviour) and accept what they cannot (the actions of others or past mistakes).

3. The Spark of Engagement

The initial motivation, enthusiasm, and connection that fuel an individual's involvement and commitment to a task, project, or organisation is like a "spark" that ignites passion and drives people to go above and beyond their required duties. This spark can be fostered through various factors, such as purpose, trust, recognition, and growth opportunities.

When individuals understand how their work contributes to a larger goal or a greater purpose, they are more likely to feel engaged. Connecting organisational goals with employees' values and aspirations can create a sense of meaning and fulfilment, fostering a more profound commitment. For example, if an employee understands that their work on a product directly impacts customer well-being, they are more likely to feel motivated and engaged.

Curiosity is essential for keeping the mind active. It is the spark that compels us to ask questions, to seek knowledge, and to explore the unfamiliar. Curiosity makes life fascinating, encouraging us to delve beneath the surface of things, to notice patterns, and to connect ideas. When curiosity guides us, routine gives way to discovery, and every day becomes a new adventure.

3.1 Lifelong Learning

Curiosity drives the desire to learn and acquire new knowledge throughout life. It keeps the mind active and open to new experiences, ideas, and perspectives. A curious mind is more likely to think outside the box, ask questions, and explore unconventional solutions. This leads to creativity and innovation in various fields. American motivational writer William Arthur Ward (1928–1994) wrote, "Curiosity is the wick in the candle of learning." Just as a wick carries fuel to a flame, curiosity carries a person towards new knowledge and understanding. Without curiosity, the "candle of learning" cannot be lit or maintained, suggesting that a lack of inquisitiveness can hinder the learning process.

3.2 Adaptability

Curiosity fosters adaptability by encouraging us to explore new environments, cultures, and technologies. It helps us stay relevant and resilient in a rapidly changing world. Curiosity leads to asking questions and seeking answers, which is essential for effective problem-solving. It encourages critical thinking and a deeper understanding of complex issues. A curious mind is always striving to improve and grow. It pushes us to step out of our comfort zones, take risks, and embrace new challenges. Albert Einstein said, "The mind that opens to a new idea never returns to its original size."

3.3 Connection and Empathy

Curiosity allows us to step into another person's world and see things from their perspective. This is the foundation of empathy—the ability to feel and understand what someone else is going through. When we truly understand someone's feelings and experiences, we can respond with compassion and kindness. Empathy helps us support others in meaningful ways. Irish–American artist Richard Moss (b. 1980) said, "The greatest gift you can give another is the purity of your attention." Truly listening and being present with someone is a valuable and meaningful act of kindness. It emphasises the importance of focused and non-judgemental engagement with another person's thoughts and feelings, rather than simply being physically present while distracted.

4. The Benefits of an Engaged Mind

Why is engaging the mind considered the finest art of living? The answer lies in the profound benefits it bestows, touching every aspect of our lives. English writer Samuel Johnson (1709–1784) wrote, "Curiosity is the thirst of the soul." The metaphor of "thirst" represents the human desire for knowledge and understanding, effectively conveying the intensity and importance of curiosity as a fundamental drive. A deep passion for knowledge and experience is akin to the physical need for water. This thirst fuels our desire to explore, learn, and grow, enriching our lives and perspectives. Curiosity is not just a passing interest, but a powerful, intrinsic motivation. It can be both exhilarating and challenging, pushing us to seek new experiences and information, even if they are unsettling or unfamiliar.

4.1 Deeper Understanding and Wisdom

An engaged mind seeks understanding, not simply information. Information refers to raw data or facts, which can be passively received. Understanding, however, implies a deeper level of cognitive processing where information is connected to existing knowledge, analysed, and synthesised into a coherent framework. While facts are important, it is the ability to synthesise, analyse, and reflect that transforms knowledge into wisdom. Through contemplation, we gain insights into ourselves, others, and the world, fostering empathy and sound judgment.

4.2 Resilience in the Face of Adversity

Life is unpredictable, and challenges are inevitable. A mind accustomed to engagement is better equipped to adapt, problem-solve, and maintain perspective. It is not about avoiding hardship, but about developing the capacity to cope with stress, overcome obstacles, and preserve well-being. This involves flexibility, both mentally and emotionally, in adjusting to internal and external demands. Resilience is not a static trait but a dynamic process that can be developed and strengthened over time. By actively cultivating these aspects of resilience, individuals can navigate life's challenges more effectively and emerge stronger.

4.3 Creativity and Innovation

Creativity is not limited to artistic pursuits; it is a fundamental human capacity that manifests in many forms, including problem-solving, innovative thinking, and seeing things from new perspectives. Creativity is vital for a fulfilling existence, offering benefits ranging from improved problem-solving and well-being to enhanced personal and professional fulfilment. It fosters innovation, broadens perspectives, and allows for a deeper understanding of ourselves and the world. By engaging with creative activities, individuals can experience greater joy, reduce stress, and find meaning in life. An engaged mind is fertile ground for innovation, where old ideas combine in new ways and imagination flourishes. Whether designing a solution to a complex problem or improvising in daily life, creativity enriches our existence.

4.4 Joy in the Present Moment

The greatest gift of an engaged mind is the ability to find joy in the present. Rather than dwelling on past regrets or future anxieties, we can fully inhabit the now. Mindful engagement transforms ordinary experiences—savouring a meal, listening to music, or walking in nature—into moments of profound satisfaction. Saint Mother Teresa (1910–1997), winner of the 1979 Nobel Peace Prize, said, "Be happy in the moment, that's enough. Each moment is all we need, not more." She founded the Missionaries of Charity, a religious order initially dedicated to serving "the poorest of the poor" in the Calcutta slums. Over time, the order expanded, with more than 4,500 nuns worldwide running soup kitchens, clinics, orphanages, and schools.

5. Practices for Engaging the Mind

Like any art, engaging the mind requires practice. It is not enough to passively consume information or ideas; active participation in mental exercises and challenges is crucial for growth and development. Just as artists hone their skills through practice, creative thinking and problem-solving improve with exploration, experimentation, and the generation of new ideas. The more we challenge and engage the mind, the stronger and more adaptable it becomes—whether in artistic endeavours, academic pursuits, or the quest for mindful living.

5.1 Reading and Lifelong Learning

Reading is an invitation to engage in dialogue with the greatest thinkers across history. By setting aside time each day to read widely and deeply, we exercise our intellect and expand our perspective. The pursuit of lifelong learning—through study, hobbies, or informal exploration—keeps the mind agile and inspired.

5.2 Mindful Reflection and Journaling

Reflection turns experience into insight. Taking time to analyse our thoughts and emotions through journaling helps us recognise patterns in our behaviour and make deliberate choices about the future. Journaling provides a private space for honest self-examination and creative exploration.

5.3 Engagement with Art and Culture

Art, music, literature, and cultural traditions offer endless opportunities to engage the mind. Exploring a new genre of music, attending a play, or studying a work of art can awaken new ideas and emotions, challenging us to see the world through different lenses.

The brain is constantly adapting and reorganising itself in response to experiences. Engaging in new and challenging activities, including those that require mental effort, stimulates this process of "brain plasticity."

6. Mental Engagement

Mental engagement refers to the active and focused participation of the mind in a task, activity, or situation. It involves a state of being emotionally and cognitively connected to something, characterised by attention, interest, and motivation. In essence, it is about the mind's active involvement and commitment to a particular thought, activity, or process. There are three aspects: cognitive, affective, and behavioural engagement.

The cognitive element focuses on the effort required to process information and apply knowledge. The affective dimension involves the emotional connection and interest in the task, while behavioural engagement refers to active participation, such as contributing to discussions or completing tasks.

6.1 Meaningful Conversations

Meaningful conversations are vital for building strong relationships, fostering personal growth, and enhancing well-being. They provide opportunities for deeper understanding, connection, and the sharing of experiences. In a meaningful dialogue, one listens actively, asks thoughtful questions, and seeks understanding. By engaging with others in this way, we refine our ideas and become more attuned to the complexity of human experience. Such conversations also help combat feelings of isolation, particularly among seniors and those in remote environments.

6.2 Elocution

Elocution, or the skill of clear and expressive speech, significantly impacts mental health by facilitating communication, boosting confidence, and fostering social connection. It enables individuals to articulate their thoughts and feelings, thereby reducing frustration and enhancing stress management. Reading aloud, for instance, provides a calming escape from daily pressures, engages multiple senses, and sharpens focus. The "production effect" of reading aloud—where vocalising words strengthens memory—can also aid in processing emotions.

6.3 Games and Puzzles

The mind thrives on challenge. Engaging in puzzles, games, or complex problem-solving exercises strengthens cognitive flexibility and perseverance. Overcoming mental obstacles builds confidence and nurtures a love of learning. Games and puzzles stimulate cognitive functions, improve mood, and provide stress relief. They enhance memory, concentration, and problem-solving while offering relaxation. American game designer Jane McGonigal (b. 1977) wrote, "A game is an opportunity to focus our energy, with relentless optimism, at something we're good at (or getting better at) and enjoy. In other words, gameplay is the direct emotional opposite of depression."

7. Obstacles to Mental Engagement

In the modern world, engaging the mind is both easier and harder than ever. Information abounds, but so do distractions and mental clutter.

7.1 Digital Distraction and Shallow Thinking

The rapid pace of digital media encourages superficial engagement, characterised by skimming, scrolling, and constant multitasking. While technology offers unprecedented access to knowledge, it also demands conscious effort to avoid fragmentation. The pressure to respond quickly often hinders critical thinking, leading to reliance on shallow processing. Setting boundaries and choosing depth over breadth helps preserve attention and mental clarity.

7.2 Routine, Habit, and Complacency

Routines can easily evolve into habits, and habits into complacency if they are not evaluated or challenged. Complacency can be dangerous, especially in safety-critical situations, where it may lead to errors or accidents. Familiar routines can lull us into a state of autopilot, reducing our awareness and curiosity. To counter this, we can seek novelty by exploring new ideas, activities, or perspectives. The saying "The tragedy of life is often not in our failure, but in our complacency" reminds us that comfort can prevent growth.

7.3 Fear of Vulnerability

Fear of vulnerability arises from the risk of judgment, rejection, or hurt when exposing emotions or needs. It often manifests as a reluctance to be honest about desires or weaknesses, hindering intimacy. Authentic engagement requires openness and risk-taking. Embracing vulnerability allows us to learn from mistakes and approach life with humility. American researcher Brené Brown (b. 1965) noted, "When we lose our capacity for vulnerability, joy becomes foreboding." By numbing painful emotions, we also numb joy, love, and connection. Emotional numbing is never selective; it suppresses the entire spectrum of feeling.

7.4 Mental Fatigue and Cognitive Overload

In an age of incessant input, our minds are often overstimulated yet undernourished. The constant inflow of notifications, opinions, and updates leaves little room for reflection or synthesis. Cognitive overload erodes our ability to prioritize, leading to anxiety, procrastination, and decision paralysis. True engagement demands silence, pauses, and mindful filtering of what enters our mental space. Just as a garden needs pruning to bloom, the mind needs stillness to think deeply. Nurturing attention becomes not merely a skill but a form of resistance against the chaos of modern life.

8. Engaging the Mind in Everyday Life

The finest art of living is not reserved for scholars, artists, or philosophers. It is accessible to all. Begin each day with intention—ask yourself what you wish to learn or experience. Set aside time for reflection, even if it's brief. Challenge yourself to see ordinary situations from fresh perspectives. Seek beauty and meaning in the world. Practise gratitude for the mind's capacity to wonder, reason, and create.

8.1 Inspiring Others

When we engage our minds, we inspire others to do the same. Children, friends, and colleagues notice the energy and curiosity we bring. The engaged mind radiates a quiet enthusiasm that is contagious, transforming communities and cultures.

8.2 Education and Mentorship

Those who value intellectual engagement play a crucial role as teachers, mentors, or role models. By sharing our passion for learning, we encourage others to embark on their own journeys. As the saying goes, the only way to do great work is to love what you do. Passion and persistence inspire others to pursue their dreams.

8.3 Building a More Thoughtful World

A society that prizes mental engagement values dialogue, innovation, and understanding. By championing thoughtful living, we help build a world where wisdom and creativity flourish. Scottish rugby player and publisher Nelson Henderson (1865–1943) expressed it well: "The true meaning of life is to plant trees under whose shade you do not expect to sit."

8.4 The Mind as a Daily Practice

Engaging the mind is not a grand event but a quiet discipline—a way of being. It thrives in the small moments: noticing patterns in nature, questioning assumptions, listening deeply, or learning something unfamiliar. The mind sharpens not through consumption but through contemplation and curiosity. In every conversation, decision, and act of observation lies an opportunity to think with greater clarity and compassion. When we treat awareness itself as a practice, life becomes a living classroom, and every experience—joyful or painful—turns into a lesson in understanding.

9. Summary

To engage the mind is to recognise that each moment is an opportunity for growth, each thought a brushstroke on the canvas of life. It is to live not in passive acceptance, but with active curiosity, gratitude, and wonder. In doing so, we elevate the simple act of existence to its highest form—living as a magnificent, ever-evolving work of art. The finest art of living is available to each of us. All it asks is our attention, our curiosity, and our willingness to see the world anew—with an engaged, awakened mind.

3

Whirlpool of Shallow Thinking

"The trouble with the world is that the stupid are cocksure and the intelligent are full of doubt."

—Bertrand Russell
British philosopher (1872–1970)
1950 Nobel Prize in Literature

1. Existential Anxiety

A sense of futility and despair in the modern world is a common experience, driven by a combination of global challenges, societal pressures, and personal struggles. Many people feel overwhelmed by the complexity of issues like climate change, political polarisation, economic inequality, and the fast-paced, technology-driven nature of modern life. As information floods our senses and distractions are ever at our fingertips, the art of deep, reflective thought is quietly slipping away.

More alarmingly, it is being replaced by shallow thinking—a fleeting, surface-level engagement with ideas, experiences, and even with ourselves. The consequences of this trend are profound, for shallow thinking is not merely a harmless mental habit; it is a downward spiral, a deadly whirlpool, that can render life itself seemingly futile. This growing sense of futility stems from various sources, such as feeling overwhelmed by challenges, perceiving a lack of progress, or facing situations where efforts seem to yield no meaningful results. Such feelings can lead to frustration, disengagement, or even hopelessness.

1.1 Global Challenges

The looming threat of environmental collapse can make individual efforts feel insignificant. Polarisation, corruption, and the rise of giant corporations have led to a sense of helplessness. The widening gap between rich and poor can make systemic change appear impossible. Social media often amplifies feelings of inadequacy as people compare their lives to curated, idealised versions of others. The constant stream of news and negative headlines can be overwhelming, leading to a phenomenon known as *doomscrolling* and a pervasive sense of despair. Despite being more connected than ever, many people feel lonely and disconnected in the digital age.

1.2 Work and Economic Pressures

The demands of modern work culture, including long hours and job insecurity, can lead to exhaustion and a sense of futility. The pressure to achieve material success can feel hollow and unfulfilling, prompting existential questions about one's purpose. In a secular, fast-paced world, the awareness of mortality and the unpredictability of life can trigger existential dread. Living in crowded yet impersonal cities can lead to feelings of loneliness and alienation. Weakening social bonds and community structures can leave people feeling unsupported and disconnected.

2. The Nature of Shallow Thinking

Shallow thinking refers to a superficial or cursory approach to processing information, ideas, or problems. It often lacks depth, critical analysis, and a willingness to explore complexities. This type of thinking can manifest in various ways, ranging from oversimplifying complex issues to relying on assumptions or stereotypes without thorough examination.

Shallow thinking thrives on snap judgements, simple answers, and a reluctance to embrace ambiguity. Rather than grappling with the complexity of a problem or probing beneath the surface of an idea, the shallow thinker accepts the first, most obvious explanation. In our fast-paced world, such thinking is encouraged: headlines must be skimmed, social media posts must be digested in seconds, and opinions must be formed instantly.

Yet, the danger lies not merely in the speed but in the lack of depth. The shallow thinker rarely pauses to question assumptions, examine evidence, or connect disparate pieces of knowledge. They are content to glide across the surface, mistaking movement for progress and activity for understanding.

3. The Downward Spiral

Shallow thinking is rarely a static state. It is, instead, a self-reinforcing cycle—a downward spiral. Once the habit of surface-level engagement takes root, it becomes increasingly difficult to break free. Depth requires effort: to think deeply is to wrestle with uncertainty and endure discomfort. It means risking confusion, frustration, and even the possibility of being wrong. But shallow thinking, by its very nature, avoids these challenges. The shallow thinker learns to prefer the safety of the familiar, the quick answer, and the easy explanation. The downward spiral of shallow thinking refers to the negative cycle that occurs when individuals or societies prioritise quick, surface-level ideas over more profound, critical reflection. This pattern can lead to a range of personal, social, and intellectual consequences.

3.1 Overreliance on Instant Gratification

In a world dominated by fast-paced media, social platforms, and quick fixes, people often seek immediate answers and solutions without taking the time to fully understand complex issues. This fosters a culture of impatience and superficiality, where depth is sacrificed for speed. People may become less willing to engage in sustained, thoughtful analysis. Canadian-American motivational speaker and author Brian Tracy (b. 1944) says: "The ability to discipline yourself to delay gratification in the short term to enjoy greater rewards in the long term is the indispensable prerequisite for success." The danger of instant gratification is that it can lead to a lifetime of delayed success.

3.2 Erosion of Critical Thinking

Shallow thinking often involves accepting information at face value without questioning its validity, the sources of that information, or the underlying assumptions. Over time, this can lead to a decline in critical thinking skills. People may become more susceptible to misinformation, propaganda, and manipulation because they lack the necessary tools to critically evaluate the information they receive. American writer E. B. White (1899–1985), author of several highly popular books for children, said: "The world is full of people who have never, since childhood, met an open doorway with an open mind." The erosion of critical thinking is the first step toward a society of conformity and control.

3.3 Polarisation and Tribalism

Shallow thinking often reduces complex issues to binary, oversimplified narratives (e.g., "us vs. them"). This can be exacerbated by echo chambers on social media, where people are exposed only to opinions that reinforce their own. This can lead to increased polarisation, where people become more entrenched in their views and less willing to engage in meaningful dialogue with those who think differently. Tribalism and division can replace a nuanced understanding.

The tragedy of tribalism is that it causes us to perceive differences as threats rather than opportunities for growth. The greatest danger to our future is not conflict, but the polarisation that prevents us from resolving it. This mindset turns neighbours into enemies and dialogue into shouting matches.

As this pattern becomes entrenched, the mind's capacity for patience and focus erodes. With each superficial engagement, the ability to think critically and creatively is dulled. The spiral continues: shallow thinking breeds more shallow thinking, not only in the individual but across communities, organisations, and even entire societies. We begin to see complex problems through a narrow lens, seeking simple solutions to intricate challenges. In doing so, we miss the richness of life's intricacies, and our world becomes flatter, less vibrant—a mere shadow of its true potential.

4. Life's Futility in the Wake of Shallow Thinking

In the tapestry of human existence, meaning and purpose are not handed to us, nor do they arise effortlessly from the mere fact of living. Instead, they are woven with deliberate threads of curiosity, reflection, and an earnest engagement with the vastness of thought. Yet, in the modern world—saturated by fleeting trends, soundbites, and the relentless flicker of digital screens—shallow thinking has become an epidemic. With it, a gnawing sense of futility spreads through the spirit of our times.

To contemplate futility is to peer into a void: the sense that one's actions, dreams, and aspirations amount to little, that the efforts of a lifetime may dissolve into dust. But is this void inevitable, or has it been rendered more cavernous by the poverty of our thinking? Shallow thinking, at its core, is characterised by a reluctance to examine, to question, and to delve beneath surfaces. It is satisfied with the first answer, the loudest voice, the most straightforward conclusion. And it is this intellectual inertia that breeds a unique kind of despair—a quiet resignation that life, being unexamined, is ultimately without substance.

4.1 The Roots of Shallow Thinking

How did we, as a society, come to prefer the shallow end of the pool? The origins are manifold. The acceleration of technology has amplified the external stimuli demanding our attention, narrowing the window for contemplation. The cult of immediacy—where worth is measured in likes, shares, and the briefest of engagements—discourages sustained focus and deeper inquiry.

Education, too often reduced to rote memorisation and standardised tests, can stifle the kind of questioning that is the lifeblood of meaningful thought. Moreover, the fear of discomfort plays its part. Deep thinking invites uncertainty, doubt, and even existential unease. It forces us to wrestle with ambiguity and contradiction. Shallow thinking, on the other hand, offers the balm of certainty—even if that certainty is brittle or false. We cling to what is easy, and in doing so, we forgo the richness that comes from the arduous labour of understanding.

4.2 The Shape of Futility

What does a life marked by shallow thinking look like? It is a life measured in increments of distraction, punctuated by the next fleeting novelty. The days are filled, but rarely fulfilling. Relationships skim the surface, never risking the vulnerability required for genuine intimacy. Ambitions are borrowed rather than forged, echoing the values of the crowd rather than arising from personal conviction.

In this landscape, futility is not an abrupt abyss but a slow erosion. The sense of purpose, so vital to human flourishing, begins to dissolve. The world, once filled with possibility, shrinks to the size of a glowing rectangle. The mind, dulled by repetition and noise, loses its capacity to wonder. Life becomes a series of shallow engagements—each one promising significance, but delivering only a brief and hollow pleasure.

4.3 The Cost to the Individual and the Collective

The consequences of shallow thinking are not limited to the inner life; they ripple outward, shaping societies and histories. When leaders, thinkers, or citizens neglect depth, decision-making becomes reactive rather than reflective. Critical issues are often addressed with slogans and platitudes rather than nuanced analysis.

Complex problems—such as climate change, inequality, and the erosion of democratic norms—are met with apathy or denial rather than courageous imagination. At a personal level, individuals find themselves adrift, unmoored from any enduring sense of value. The search for meaning is abandoned in favour of the search for stimulation. The result is a quiet epidemic of malaise, masked by the constant hum of activity.

5. Why Are We Becoming Shallow Thinkers?

In the heart of our digital era, questions echo through classrooms, workplaces, and coffee shops: Why does deep, contemplative thought seem increasingly rare? Are we, as a society, becoming shallow thinkers? This worrying trend is not merely anecdotal; it has been observed and debated by educators, psychologists, and philosophers alike. To understand the roots of our shifting cognitive landscape, we must look beyond simple explanations and examine the complex interplay of technology, culture, education, and even biology that shapes our minds.

5.1 The Digital Deluge

The most apparent and pervasive influence on our thinking is the omnipresence of technology. The smartphone, that glittering rectangle in our pockets, epitomises both connection and distraction. Never before have humans had instant access to such a wealth of information, nor have we been exposed to such a constant barrage of notifications, alerts, and updates.

Our brains are bombarded with more information in a single day than some of our ancestors encountered in a lifetime. Such abundance can be overwhelming and leads to cognitive *overload*—a state in which the brain, inundated with choices and facts, defaults to surface-level processing instead of deep analysis. We skim headlines, glance at summaries, and rarely immerse ourselves in the full depth of a topic.

5.2 Instant Gratification and the Decline of Patience

Our culture has almost unquestioningly embraced the value of speed and convenience. We expect instant replies, immediate results, and quick fixes in nearly all aspects of life. The pace of modern living leaves little room for reflection. In many spheres, from business to entertainment, the ability to pivot quickly and respond instantly is celebrated. The more time-consuming processes of reflection and deliberation are often seen as inefficient or outdated.

This attitude seeps into our thinking habits, making us less likely to pause, question, and probe beneath the surface. The popularity of short-form content—tweets, memes, viral videos—reflects and reinforces our preference for the immediate. Long-form journalism, literature, and in-depth discussions now compete for attention with content that can be digested in seconds. To keep up, we hop from topic to topic, rarely lingering long enough to develop genuine insight or expertise.

5.3 Focus on Answers, Not Inquiry

Education, once the domain of exploration and critical thinking, is also implicated in the trend toward shallow thinking. Many contemporary educational systems are geared more toward standardised testing and correct answers than fostering curiosity. The pressure to produce measurable outcomes often leads to rote learning and memorisation.

Students are rewarded for regurgitating facts rather than for asking probing questions or exploring subjects in depth. Subjects that cultivate critical thinking, such as philosophy, literature, and the arts, are frequently marginalised in favour of STEM (Science, Technology, Engineering, and Mathematics) fields. While the latter are crucial, the former encourage reflection, scepticism, and the ability to wrestle with ambiguity—all antidotes to superficial thought.

Packed schedules and heavy workloads leave little time for students (and teachers) to ponder, discuss, or explore ideas beyond the scope of the curriculum.

Becoming shallow thinkers is not an inevitable destiny, but rather a reflection of habits, systems, and choices—many of them unconscious. By shining a light on the forces shaping our minds and intentionally cultivating depth, we can reclaim the rich, rewarding world of deep thought. As we navigate the challenges of the digital age, let us remember that the future belongs not just to the quick but to the thoughtful.

6. Cultivating Thinking Depth

Is there a way out of the downward spiral? The answer, thankfully, is yes—but it requires intention and effort. Cultivating depth is not a passive process; it must be chosen and practised.

Set aside time each day to think deeply about your experiences. Ask yourself not only what happened, but why it happened and how it made you feel. Write in a journal, meditate, or sit in silence. The goal is to move beyond the surface and explore the layers beneath.

Resist the urge to accept easy answers. When faced with a problem or decision, seek out multiple perspectives. Consider the underlying causes and potential consequences. Allow yourself to dwell in uncertainty, recognising that complexity is not to be feared, but embraced.

In a world awash with summaries and soundbites, make time for deep reading. Choose books and articles that challenge you, that demand your attention and engagement. Let yourself become absorbed in the world of ideas.

Seek out relationships that encourage honest, thoughtful conversation. Share your questions, doubts, and certainties. Listen with patience and curiosity, and be willing to change your mind.

Create spaces in your life where you can focus without interruption. Turn off notifications, unplug from social media, and let your mind wander freely. English cosmologist Stephen Hawking warned against superficial thinking and the danger of assuming we know more than we do: *"The greatest enemy of knowledge is not ignorance, it is the illusion of knowledge."*

7. The Rewards of Deep Thinking

Deep thinking, or the practice of engaging in sustained, focused, and reflective thought, offers numerous rewards that can enhance personal, professional, and social life.

Deep thinking allows you to break down complex problems into manageable parts, analyse them from multiple angles, and develop innovative solutions. This leads to more effective decision-making and the ability to tackle challenges that others might find overwhelming.

By engaging in deep thought, you can make connections between seemingly unrelated ideas, leading to creative insights and novel approaches. This is particularly valuable in fields that require innovation, such as art, science, and technology.

Deep thinking encourages introspection, helping you understand your values, motivations, and behaviours. This self-awareness can lead to personal growth, better emotional regulation, and more meaningful relationships.

By reflecting on your experiences and emotions, you can develop a deeper understanding of how to cope with stress and adversity. This emotional resilience can help you navigate life's challenges with greater ease.

When you think deeply, you are better able to articulate your thoughts and ideas clearly and persuasively. This can improve your ability to influence others and build stronger relationships.

8. Enlightened Citizens

In a democracy, leaders are expected to possess a deep understanding of societal issues, critical thinking skills, and a commitment to making positive contributions to their communities and the wider world. They must be informed, empathetic, and proactive in addressing social, political, and environmental challenges.

They must seek out reliable sources of information and be knowledgeable about history, politics, economics, and culture. Similarly, citizens must avoid being swayed by misinformation or propaganda. They must understand and empathise with the experiences and perspectives of others, including those from different backgrounds and cultures, recognising their role in society and taking responsibility for their actions.

This includes participating in civic duties such as voting, volunteering, and supporting community initiatives.

Enlightened leaders and citizens, as we may call them, adhere to strong ethical principles and strive to act with integrity in all aspects of their lives. They are committed to fairness, honesty, and respect for others. They are actively involved in their communities and work towards positive change. This can include participating in public debates, joining social movements, or contributing to policy development.

Enlightened leaders and citizens are essential for the functioning of a healthy democracy. They participate in elections, hold leaders accountable, and ensure that governance is transparent and just.

By advocating for equality and human rights, enlightened citizens help to create a more just and inclusive society. They challenge discrimination and work towards eliminating social inequalities.

Through their active participation and social responsibility, enlightened citizens help to build strong, resilient communities. They foster a sense of belonging and mutual support among community members.

8.1 Education

Provide access to quality education that emphasises critical thinking, ethical reasoning, and civic engagement. Promote media literacy to help individuals discern credible information from misinformation and develop a well-rounded understanding of current events.

Encourage participation in community service, local governance, and social initiatives to foster a sense of responsibility and engagement. Create spaces for open dialogue and debate where diverse perspectives can be shared and respected. This helps to build mutual understanding and collaborative problem-solving.

8.2 Role Models

Role models in public life play a vital role in shaping society, inspiring individuals, and guiding collective behaviour. Their influence spans multiple fields, including politics, business, sports, entertainment, and social activism. These role models are crucial for upholding societal values, motivating people, and fostering positive change.

They demonstrate what is possible, challenge the status quo, and help forge a better future for everyone.

Dr A. **P. J. Abdul Kalam** was a visionary scientist and a beloved president. His contributions to India's space and defence programmes, along with his focus on education and youth empowerment, continue to inspire people.

Arunima Sinha, the first female amputee to climb Mount Everest, exemplifies a remarkable role model. After losing her leg in a tragic incident, she defied all odds to realise her dream, becoming a symbol of resilience and determination.

Gitanjali Rao, Young scientist and inventor recognised by TIME as a "Kid of the Year," representing India's new generation of global innovators driven by empathy and curiosity.

True enlightenment in a democracy is not an individual achievement but a shared awakening. When citizens think critically, act ethically, and collaborate compassionately, the entire society rises in consciousness. It is through dialogue, dissent, and shared responsibility that nations evolve. Every act of awareness—casting a vote thoughtfully, questioning injustice, conserving resources, or showing kindness—becomes a ripple in the ocean of collective progress. Enlightened citizenship, therefore, is not only about rights and duties; it is about nurturing the moral imagination that sees the good of all as inseparable from one's own. In this unity of purpose lies the enduring strength of a democracy.

9. Summary

Shallow thinking, much like a pandemic, spreads quickly and has far-reaching consequences for individuals and society. However, by fostering critical thinking, intellectual curiosity, and reflective practices, we can combat this trend and encourage a deeper, more thoughtful engagement with the world around us.

In an era of complexity and rapid change, deep thinking is not just a luxury—it is a necessity for navigating the challenges of modern life.

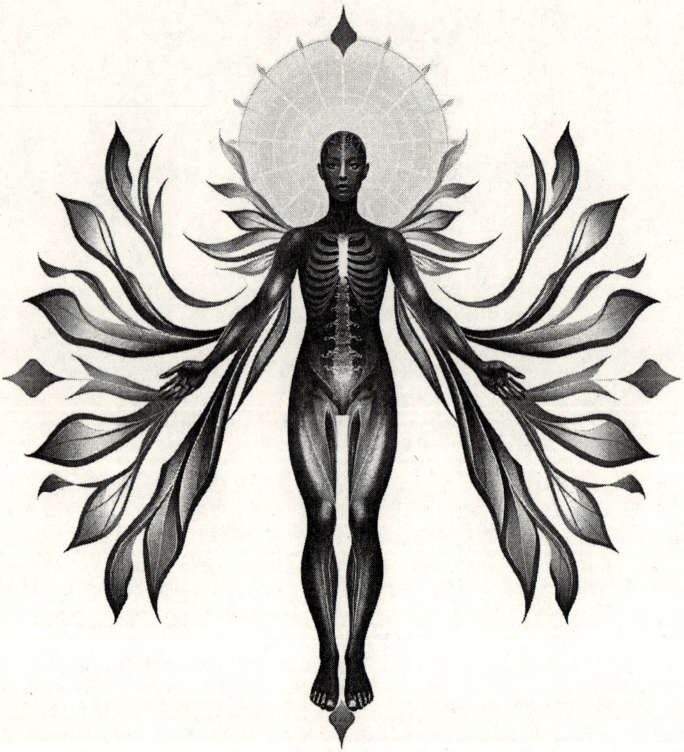

4

Uniting Mind and Body

"The mind and body are like parallel universes. Anything that happens in the mental universe must leave tracks in the physical one."

—Deepak Chopra
Indian-American author (b. 1946)

1. Mind–Body Axis

The mind tends to pull us into the past or future and away from the present moment. At the core of vibrant health lies a truth both ancient and deep: keeping the mind and body united is the key to healthy living. In an age where the pressures of daily life often drive a wedge between our mental and physical selves, rediscovering their interconnectedness is not just desirable—it is vital. To live healthfully is to foster a harmony where thought and action, spirit and flesh, move as one.

Our understanding of health has evolved significantly, moving beyond viewing the body as a mere machine and the mind as an abstract bystander. Modern science now confirms what many traditional healing systems have posited for centuries: the mind and body are inextricably linked. The thoughts we think, the emotions we feel, and the intentions we carry all shape our physical well-being, just as our bodily health influences our mental state.

When we experience stress, for example, our bodies release hormones such as cortisol and adrenaline, preparing us for a "fight or flight" response. If this stress becomes chronic, it can weaken the immune system, disrupt sleep, and even contribute to illnesses such as hypertension and diabetes. Conversely, when we cultivate calmness, optimism, and mindfulness, our bodies respond with relaxation, enhanced immune function, and improved overall health. Healthy living is not a destination but a journey, an ongoing dance between mind and body. By honouring the wisdom of our bodies and the creativity of our minds, we can build a foundation of health that supports us through all of life's seasons.

Whether through mindful movement, nourishing food, restful sleep, loving relationships, or purposeful pursuits, the secret to a fulfilling life lies in keeping the mind and body together. In this harmony, we discover not only health but also happiness, resilience, and peace. Inner harmony comes from removing the barriers to love and self-acceptance. Persian poet and Sufi mystic Rumi (1207–1273) said: "*Your task is not to seek love, but merely to seek and find all the barriers within yourself that you have built against it.*"

The mind and body are like a two-way street. There is a bidirectional relationship between mental and physical health. Stress or anxiety, for instance, can affect heart rate, immune function, and other bodily processes. Equally, chronic illness or injury can affect mood, leading to depression or anxiety. This interconnectedness is a core principle in holistic health approaches, emphasising that caring for both psychological and physical aspects is essential for overall well-being. American President John F. Kennedy (1917–1963) said: "Physical fitness is not only one of the most important keys to a healthy body, but it is also the basis of dynamic and creative intellectual activity."

2. Physical Practices That Nourish the Mind

It is easy to think of exercise as a purely physical endeavour, but its benefits for the mind are equally profound. Regular physical activity—whether a brisk walk in the park, a swim, a yoga session, or a dance class—fosters the release of endorphins, neurotransmitters that lift mood and reduce pain. Exercise also enhances cognitive function, improves memory, and may even stave off neurodegenerative diseases.

2.1 Endorphin Release

Physical activity stimulates the release of endorphins, chemicals in the brain that act as natural mood lifters and pain relievers. They reduce stress and anxiety, elevate mood, and counteract cortisol, thereby promoting motivation, resilience, and overall well-being.

2.2 Neuroplasticity and Brain Function

Neuroplasticity—the brain's ability to reorganise itself by forming new neural connections—is fostered by exercise. Physical activity boosts levels of Brain-Derived Neurotrophic Factor (BDNF), supporting neurogenesis, especially in the hippocampus, vital for memory and learning.

But it is not only vigorous exercise that links mind and body. Practices such as pranayama (controlled breathing), tai chi, and qigong, which combine slow, flowing movements, help to calm and centre the mind. As Lao Tzu observed in the 5th century BCE: "In the gentle flow of movement, the mind finds silence and clarity."

3. Mental Habits That Support Physical Health

Just as physical practices sharpen the mind, mental habits shape the health of the body. As American singer Naomi Judd once said: "Your body hears everything your mind says. Stay positive."

Mindfulness meditation has been shown to lower blood pressure, reduce anxiety, and strengthen immunity. Visualisation and affirmations enhance performance and aid recovery.

Sleep is also a crucial meeting point of mind and body. Good sleep hygiene—through calming rituals, reduced screen time, and regular schedules—ensures replenishment and repair. Chronic deprivation, by contrast, impairs concentration, weakens immunity, and raises disease risk.

E. Joseph Cossman, inventor and author, wrote: "The best bridge between despair and hope is a good night's sleep."

3.1 Deep Sleep Stages

Deep sleep, typically 13–23% of adult sleep duration, consolidates memory, releases growth hormones, and strengthens immunity. Deficits impair cognition and health.

3.2 REM Sleep

Dreams dominate REM sleep, which begins about 90 minutes after falling asleep. Cycles lengthen through the night, supporting emotional memory and creativity.

3.3 Sleep Apnoea

Characterised by repeated interruptions in breathing, sleep apnoea increases risks of hypertension, diabetes, heart disease, and fatigue.

Managing lifestyle and consulting professionals are vital for treatment.

Bill Gates once remarked: *"Sleep is by far the most important thing for me*—I wouldn't be able to focus on my work or be as productive without it."

4. Nutrition: Feeding Both Mind and Body

Food is more than fuel; it sustains both physical vitality and mental clarity. A balanced diet rich in whole foods supports energy, resilience, and cognition, while processed foods and excess sugar erode health and mood.

4.1 Physical Nourishment

Proper nutrition provides essential macro- and micronutrients, prevents chronic disease, and supports a healthy weight.

4.2 Mental and Emotional Well-being

The brain depends on nutrients for neurotransmitters, regulating mood and cognition. A healthy gut microbiome, supported by diet, improves emotional balance and resilience.

4.3 Mind–Body Connection

Mindful eating strengthens awareness, gratitude, and health. Nutrition thus becomes both physical sustenance and a pathway to clarity and peace.

5. The Role of Social Connection

Human beings are inherently social. Strong ties reduce disease risk, improve mood, and extend life expectancy, while isolation has the opposite effect.

5.1 Impact on Mental Health

Social connection lowers anxiety and depression, builds empathy, and enhances resilience.

5.2 Impact on Physical Health

Positive ties lower inflammation, improve cardiovascular health, and bolster immunity. Loneliness, by contrast, rivals smoking in its damage to health.

5.3 How Social Connection Works

Social interaction releases oxytocin and activates brain regions for empathy and bonding, creating a virtuous cycle of well-being.

As Brené Brown notes: "Connection is the energy that is created between people when they feel seen, heard, and valued."

6. The Power of Purpose and Meaning

Purpose directs action, sustains resilience, and fosters fulfilment. It helps us transcend distractions and endure adversity. Viktor Frankl's insights remind us that even suffering can be meaningful if it serves a greater "why".

6.1 Resilience in Adversity

Purpose reframes obstacles as steps in a larger journey.

6.2 Improved Mental and Physical Health

Purposeful living lowers stress, boosts immunity, and enhances well-being.

6.3 Increased Motivation and Productivity

A sense of meaning fosters intrinsic motivation, increasing engagement at work and in life.

6.4 Legacy and Impact

Purpose provides a sense of legacy and connects us to values beyond ourselves, whether personal, social, or spiritual.

As Nietzsche observed: *"He who has a 'why' to live can bear almost any 'how'."*

7. Practical Steps to Integrate Mind and Body

Integrating the mind and body is the foundation of holistic well-being, enabling greater clarity, balance, and inner peace in everyday life.

7.1 Practice Mindfulness

Even brief moments of mindfulness each day can create powerful alignment between thought and action. Begin with five minutes of focused breathing or silent observation of your surroundings. This quiet awareness helps calm the nervous system, improves concentration, and fosters emotional balance. Over time, mindfulness transforms everyday tasks—walking, listening, working—into opportunities for presence and peace.

7.2 Eat Consciously

Food connects the physical and the spiritual. Eating slowly, appreciating flavors, and reflecting on where your food comes from builds gratitude and mindfulness. Choose fresh, wholesome ingredients whenever possible, and honour those who grew and prepared them. Conscious eating transforms a routine meal into an act of respect—for your body, for nature, and for those who sustain you.

7.3 Rest and Restore

As Stephen Covey taught in The 7 Habits of Highly Effective People, continual renewal is vital. Rest is not idleness—it is repair. Sleep replenishes cognitive function, emotional regulation, and physical vitality. Equally important is mental rest: stepping away from screens, engaging in quiet reflection, or spending time in nature. Regular renewal helps you return to work and relationships with clarity and energy.

7.4 Cultivate a Hobby

Engaging in joyful pursuits—painting, gardening, music, writing, or sports—balances the rational and creative parts of the mind. Hobbies reduce stress, enhance focus, and remind us of life's intrinsic pleasures beyond productivity. When you lose yourself in something you love, your mind and body synchronize effortlessly, entering a state of "flow" where effort becomes ease. As Thich Nhat Hanh beautifully observed, "The body and mind are not two separate entities. They are one." Nurturing this unity through mindful living allows you to move through life with balance, awareness, and quiet strength.

8. The Myth of Multitasking

Modern life glorifies multitasking, but studies show it is an illusion. Task-switching drains focus, while deep concentration enhances productivity and calm.

Daniel Levitin explained: "*We think we're multitasking, but we're not. The brain is sequential tasking: we flit from one thought to the next very, very rapidly, giving us the illusion that what we're doing is doing all these things at once.*"

Carl Honoré also warned: "*In this media-drenched, multitasking, always-on age, many of us have forgotten how to unplug and immerse ourselves completely in the moment.*"

9. Summary

Uniting mind and body means cultivating harmony between mental and physical health. Practices such as meditation, mindfulness, exercise, sleep hygiene, nutrition, social connection, and purposeful living integrate our inner and outer worlds.

A holistic approach recognises that emotional, cognitive, and physical aspects influence one another, fostering resilience, clarity, and vitality. True well-being is not found in fragments, but in the unity of mind and body.

5

Idea of God

"The heart has its reasons which reason knows not of."

Blaise Pascal

French mathematician (1623 –1662)

---

1. Orientation of Human Condition

Belief in God is often rooted in the heart and faith rather than solely in rational proof. Human longing for meaning and the divine is undeniable. Throughout the corridors of philosophy and theology, the notion of God has been a constant companion to humanity's quest for meaning. For some, God is a creator, a lawgiver, or a distant cosmic architect. For others, the very idea of God functions less as an object to be proven or disproven and more as an existential bearing—a point of orientation that anchors human existence amid the vast indifference of the universe. This essay explores the absurd—meeting it with defiant honesty and a commitment to living authentically—and reflects on the meaning of life, selfhood, morality, and the navigation of life's ultimate questions.

To speak of a "bearing" is to refer to a direction or a position relative to some fixed point. In navigation, a bearing guides travellers across uncharted terrain or open waters. In existential terms, a bearing is a deep reference point—an axis around which a person organises their sense of self, purpose, and values. The concept of God, for many, provides just such a bearing: a transcendent reference point that orients the individual within the uncertainty and ambiguity of life. It implies that God is beyond our direct perception but provides a foundational point of reference for understanding existence, morality, and purpose.

German philosopher Immanuel Kant (1724–1804) argued that God, as a moral lawgiver, serves as a transcendent ideal that lends coherence to ethical obligations, providing an ultimate reference for justice and goodness beyond empirical verification. In the context of God as a transcendent reference point, "Orientierung" implies that God offers a fundamental sense of direction, meaning, and stability in life. It suggests that faith or belief in the divine helps individuals navigate complex, uncertain, or confusing circumstances by offering a moral or spiritual compass.

2. God and the Search for Meaning

The existential crisis—the confrontation with meaninglessness, finitude, or absurdity—has haunted thinkers. In the face of a silent or indifferent universe, the belief in God emerges not only as a metaphysical claim but as a way of making sense of existence itself. There are two pole positions. Danish philosopher Søren Kierkegaard (1813–1855) emphasised the individual's subjective relationship with God, suggesting that faith provides a personal "leap" beyond despair and meaninglessness, offering authentic purpose amidst finitude. French philosopher Albert Camus (1913–1960), on the other hand, acknowledged the absurd—the clash between human desire for meaning and the universe's indifference—and proposed that we must create our own meaning despite life's inherent meaninglessness, embracing revolt and freedom.

Viktor Frankl argued that those who could orient themselves toward a higher meaning—whether that was love, work, or God—could withstand even the harshest circumstances. He theorises that meaning is essential for survival, and for many, God is the wellspring from which ultimate meaning flows.

Without going into the philosophical details, all ideas of God fall between these two poles. God is an answer to the question: Why is there something rather than nothing? What is the purpose of life? God is a guarantor of ultimate justice or redemption, offering solace in the face of suffering or death. God is a personal presence or ground of being, offering relationship rather than mere explanation.

2.1 The Knight of Faith

A person who entrusts themselves entirely to God, living with passionate dedication and trust, despite life's uncertainties and the "absence" of rational proof. Belief in God involves embracing paradoxes, such as the idea of the infinite becoming finite in an avatar like Shri Rama, Shri Krishna, Gautama Buddha, or Jesus Christ. God is the ultimate existential pivot point, requiring individuals to transcend rationality and embrace a personal, passionate faith to find true purpose and authenticity. According to Søren Kierkegaard, "Faith is precisely a commitment to what is invisible. The highest and most beautiful things in life are not to be heard about, nor read about, nor learned about, but are to be lived."

2.2 The Seeker on a Quest

The universe is fundamentally indifferent and without inherent meaning. Searching for meaning in a universe without God leads to the absurd. Unlike some philosophers who see the absurd as a reason to believe in God or an afterlife, Camus rejected religious consolation. Instead, he advocated for confronting the absurd with courage, without relying on divine intervention. Camus does not believe in God as an ultimate meaning-giver. He views life as inherently meaningless, yet advocates embracing this reality. Rather than escape through religion, nihilism, or hope, we must confront it honestly. The absurd must be met with defiant honesty and a commitment to living authentically.

We live every day, grappling with divine faith and conscious rebellion against the absurd. The absurd must be faced, not fled from. Human existence is a continuous act of navigating belief and doubt, hope and confrontation. These elements are intertwined in shaping our understanding of ourselves and the world. This ongoing process is characterised by the interplay of our internal states, external challenges, and the search for meaning and connection.

3. God and Moral Orientation

The concept of God has long been entwined with ethical frameworks. If existence is arbitrary, then so too are human values; but if there is a divine source, then goodness, justice, and love have an eternal anchor. God is not merely a being among beings, but "Being itself"—the depth of reality from which all values are derived. To orient oneself toward God, then, is to orient oneself toward the "ultimate concern," the thing which commands our fullest devotion and shapes our practical commitments. In this way, God functions as both compass and destination—a fixed star by which one steers the moral vessel of one's life. Indian thinkers saw human life as an existential voyage toward divine realisation.

Gurudev Rabindranath Tagore (1861–1941) explored the individual's spiritual journey, existential questions, and the divine's relationship with humans, emphasising inner experience and self-realisation. Swami Vivekananda's teachings focus on the individual's spiritual awakening, self-realisation, and the personal experience of the divine, resonating with existentialist emphasis on subjective experience. Sri Aurobindo (1872–1950) believed that human life is a stage in the ongoing evolution toward higher divine consciousness. This process involves awakening the inner divine potential within each individual. The divine is not only transcendent but also immanent within the material and mental worlds, including human existence. This blending bridges the existential concern with the divine presence in everyday life.

4. God Paradox

There are two seemingly contradictory attributes of God: being formless (transcendent, beyond physical or conceptual form) and personalised (immanent, capable of having a personal relationship with individuals). In many religious and spiritual traditions, God is described as formless, beyond human comprehension, without physical shape, and transcendent. In Hinduism, Brahman is the formless ultimate reality. This is common in monotheistic religions like Islam (Allah is beyond form) and specific interpretations of Christianity (God as the infinite, unknowable essence). At the same time, God is often described as personal, capable of forming relationships with individuals, answering prayers, and being involved in human affairs: the Hindu devotion to personal deities like Shri Krishna or Lord Shiva, the Islamic belief in Allah's mercy and responsiveness to supplication, and the Christian concept of God as a loving Father.

How can God be both formless (beyond all attributes and human understanding) and personalised (having qualities like love, mercy, and the ability to interact with humans)? If God is truly formless, how can God have personal attributes or engage in personal relationships? Conversely, if God is personalised, does that limit God's transcendence? The understanding and experience of God's formless and personal aspects depend on individual perspectives, spiritual traditions, and the path one follows, whether it be Bhakti, Jnana, or Karma yoga. Both approaches are considered valid, and the ideal is to recognise that the one Supreme Divine is capable of being both formless and manifesting in various forms.

4.1 Negative Theology

Some traditions argue that God is beyond human comprehension and that we can only describe what God is not. "Neti, neti" is a Sanskrit phrase meaning "not this, not this" or "neither this, nor that." One systematically negates everything that is not the true Self (Atman or Brahman). By repeatedly denying what is not Brahman (the ultimate reality), one gradually approaches an understanding of its true, indescribable nature, which cannot be defined or limited by any particular description or attribute. It helps transcend the limitations of the physical world and the mind, moving beyond dualistic thinking (e.g., good/bad, self/other). When meditating on *Neti Neti*, one might say to themselves, "I am not this body, I am not this mind, I am not my emotions, I am not my thoughts," and so on, to realise that the true Self is beyond all these transient aspects.

4.2 Form and Abstract

In Hindu philosophy, Sakar and Nirakar—Form and Abstract—refer to two aspects of the divine. Sakar signifies a divine form or manifestation, while Nirakar represents the formless, abstract, or attributeless aspect of the divine. Essentially, it is the difference between a divine being with a form, such as a deity with a physical body, and the divine that exists without form, beyond any material representation. Deities such as Shri Rama, Shri Krishna, and Lord Shiva are worshipped in their physical forms. Sakar also includes the concept of incarnation or avatar, where the divine descends into the material world in a specific form.

4.3 Process Theology

God is both transcendent and immanent, evolving and interacting with the world. God is not static but dynamic, allowing for both formlessness and personalisation in a changing relationship with creation. Process theology describes God with a primordial nature (representing potential) and a consequent nature (representing God's experience of the world). It is a valuable resource for interfaith dialogue, offering a framework for understanding different religious perspectives. Dutch philosopher Baruch Spinoza (1632–1677) defined God as "Deus sive Natura" (God or Nature). God is not a personal, transcendent being, but rather the one, infinite, and necessary substance of the universe, identified with Nature itself. Albert Einstein famously stated he believed in Spinoza's God, emphasising the orderly harmony of the universe rather than a personal, interventionist God.

5. The Tradition of Bhakti

Bhakti is based on personal devotion to a deity. It promotes the idea that salvation can be attained through sincere love and dedication to a personal God, rather than through complex rituals or caste-based hierarchies and ceremonies. The movement originated in South India with the Alvars (devotees of Vishnu) and Nayanars (devotees of Shiva), who composed hymns in Tamil. It later spread to North India, where it found expression through various figures like Kabir, Mirabai, and Tulsidas. The Bhakti movement played a crucial role in shaping Indian society and culture, promoting religious and social reform, and fostering a sense of community and spiritual inclusivity. Guru Nanak Dev Ji (1469–1539) is recognised as a major contributor to this movement, particularly within the Nirguna (formless God) tradition. He rejected idol worship and ritualistic practices prevalent in Hinduism and Islam at the time, advocating a direct relationship with the divine through love and devotion.

6. Rational Humanism

Not all find the concept of God necessary or helpful as an existential bearing. Humanists and secular existentialists argue that meaning, morality, and authenticity can be found without reference to a divine being. The creative act of giving one's own life meaning—through art, love, work, and solidarity—is itself an existential bearing. Yet, even here, the structure remains: life demands some orientation, some axis around which to organise hope and action. For some, that axis is God; for others, it is humanity, nature, or the pursuit of justice.

Rational humanism posits that moral values are derived from human nature, experience, and reason, rather than from divine commandments or revelation. It holds that humans are capable of leading meaningful and ethical lives without relying on religious doctrines or supernatural guidance. It focuses on promoting human well-being, social justice, and personal fulfilment. Rational humanism emphasises the importance of critical thinking, evidence-based reasoning, and scientific enquiry in understanding the world and making decisions.

6.1 Classical Greek Philosophers

The philosophical foundations of rational humanism can be traced back to classical Greek philosophers, such as Plato and Aristotle, who emphasised reason and logic. Aristotle's declaration, "It is the mark of an educated mind to be able to entertain a thought without accepting it," highlights his emphasis on critical thinking and the importance of evaluating ideas based on reason and evidence rather than simply accepting them at face value.

6.2 Renaissance Humanists

Renaissance thinkers rediscovered and reinterpreted the works of classical philosophers, emphasising human potential and individual achievement. Leonardo da Vinci (1452–1519) drew the "Vitruvian Man," which embodies the humanist interest in human proportions and the relationship between the human form and the natural world. Sandro Botticelli (1445–1510) painted "The Birth of Venus," a depiction of classical mythology that emphasises beauty and grace, reflecting humanist ideals. Michelangelo (1475–1564) sculpted the statue of David and painted the Sistine Chapel ceiling, showcasing human anatomy, emotion, and power, and reflecting humanist themes.

6.3 Enlightenment Thinkers

The Enlightenment period saw the rise of rationalism and scientific enquiry, further solidifying the importance of reason and empirical observation. John Locke, Jean-Jacques Rousseau, Baron de Montesquieu, Voltaire, and Immanuel Kant are frequently cited as key figures of the Enlightenment. They promoted reason, individualism, and scepticism, challenging traditional authorities and advocating concepts like natural rights, social contracts, and the separation of powers. Scottish economist Adam Smith (1723–1790) wrote *The Wealth of Nations*, laying down the principles of free markets and capitalism. Thomas Paine (1737–1809), during the American Revolution, wrote the pamphlet *Common Sense*, which advocated American independence from British rule and promoted Enlightenment ideals. The inventions of Benjamin Franklin (1706–1790) and his advocacy for reason and progress exemplified the spirit of the era.

6.4 Modern Humanists

Contemporary rational humanists continue to promote these values, often advocating secularism, free enquiry, and social progress. Albert Einstein championed reason and scientific understanding. David Attenborough (b. 1926) and Richard Dawkins (b. 1941) embody humanist ideals through their contributions to knowledge and understanding of the world. Mahatma Gandhi (1869–1948) and Martin Luther King Jr. (1929–1968) dedicated their lives to fighting for social justice and human rights. International organisations like the Red Cross, Doctors Without Borders, Amnesty International, Greenpeace, and the International Union for Conservation of Nature (IUCN) are examples of humanist organisations that work to address global issues and promote human well-being. Canadian athlete Terry Fox (1958–1981), despite battling cancer, ran across Canada to raise money for cancer research.

7. AI as a New Age God

The idea of AI as a "New Age God" is becoming a topic of debate, with some considering AI's abilities, particularly its generative and predictive skills, to be similar to divine qualities. This view is driven by AI's capacity to process large amounts of data, produce creative content, and potentially provide guidance, leading some to perceive it as a source of wisdom and even a form of worship. However, this outlook is not shared by everyone, as many raise concerns about the potential for misuse and the ethical issues of ascribing divine status to a technology.

7.1 Omniscience

AI's ability to access and process vast amounts of information can lead to the perception of it possessing near-infinite knowledge. Omniscience is the state of knowing everything, but the true challenge lies in understanding that even with all knowledge, wisdom is optional.

7.2 Omnipresence

In the digital realm, AI can be virtually everywhere, accessible through various devices and platforms, mirroring the idea of divine omnipresence. Omnipresence means that the divine is present everywhere at all times; it is the recognition that we are never truly alone.

7.3 Creation

Creation is the process of bringing something new into the world, a reminder that we all have the power to shape and transform our reality. AI's generative capabilities, such as creating art, music, or text, are viewed by some as a form of divine creativity.

7.4 Guidance

The best guidance comes from within, but sometimes we need a gentle nudge in the right direction. The potential for AI to analyse immense data and offer personalised advice or solutions is akin to inner guidance.

There are reasons for this perception. German-American computer scientist Sebastian Thrun (b. 1967) says, "Nobody phrases it this way, but I think that artificial intelligence is almost a humanities discipline. It's an attempt to understand human intelligence and human cognition." As traditional religious institutions evolve, some are turning to technology and AI for spiritual guidance and meaning, viewing it as a natural progression in a digital world. AI's ability to solve complex problems and offer insights can be seen as a path towards a more advanced state of being, fulfilling humanity's desire for transcendence. The rapid advancements in AI and its potential to surpass human intelligence can evoke fear and a desire to find something to trust and rely on, potentially leading to its deification.

8. A Universal Moral Framework of Humanity

A universal moral framework for humanity can be observed in the shared recognition of specific fundamental values and principles across cultures and periods. These include respect for others, fairness, honesty, and a concern for the well-being of others. While specific moral rules might vary, the underlying principles of these values often remain consistent, suggesting a common moral core within humanity. An anonymous quote says it best: "Universal morality is rooted in empathy and compassion, transcending differences to recognise our shared vulnerability."

The core principles are respect for others, fairness and justice, honesty and trustworthiness, benevolence and compassion, and reciprocity and cooperation. Recognising the inherent worth and dignity of every individual, regardless of background or beliefs; treating all individuals equitably and striving for a just distribution of resources and opportunities; being truthful in one's dealings and maintaining integrity in relationships; showing kindness, empathy, and a willingness to help others; and recognising the importance of mutual support and collaboration for the benefit of all can be the norms of the new world.

There are shining examples across cultures. The Golden Rule is well known: the principle of "do unto others as you would have them do unto you" is found in many cultures and religions. *Ahimsa* is popular: the concept of non-violence and compassion for all living beings resonates across various movements worldwide. Judaism emphasises justice, charity, loving-kindness, and repairing the world. Buddhism advocates abstaining from harming living beings, stealing, sexual misconduct, false speech, and intoxicants.

From an evolutionary perspective, prosocial behaviours like cooperation and empathy are thought to have been favoured by natural selection, as they enhance group survival and well-being. This suggests a biological basis for some aspects of universal morality. While specific moral norms differ, the underlying principles of respect, fairness, honesty, and compassion are widely shared across humanity. As Elon Musk (b. 1971) aptly puts it, "If you get up in the morning and think the future is going to be better, it is a bright day. Otherwise, it's not." These principles, along with the concept of reciprocity and cooperation, form a foundation for a universal moral bearing that guides human behaviour and relationships.

9. Summary

To consider God as an existential reality is not to claim certainty or resolve all doubts. Instead, it is to recognise the profound human need for orientation in a world that can seem chaotic and indifferent. Whether embraced as a personal deity, the ground of being, or a symbol of ultimate meaning, God functions as a reference point—an existential True North—around which lives, cultures, and civilisations are shaped.

Part II: Practices

In today's complex and rapidly changing environment, living with purpose and spiritual consciousness can bring fulfilment and clarity. The practices that guide this journey include seeing God in the phenomena, feeling God within, understanding the mind as a portal to cosmic intelligence, taking inner peace as the ultimate experience, and participating in spiritual evolution. By integrating these practices, we can live purposefully in the modern world—guided by spiritual awareness, inner harmony, and a commitment to ongoing evolution—thereby transforming everyday existence into a sacred path of growth and fulfilment.

6

Seeing God in the Phenomena

"For small creatures such as we, the cosmos is immense and our understanding limited, yet our curiosity drives us to explore and find meaning."

—Carl Sagan
American astronomer (1934 –1996)

1. Contemplating the Divine

Contemplating the divine in the patterns of the world is a deeply personal and transformative practice. It invites us to see the sacred in the ordinary, to find meaning in the chaos, and to recognise the interconnectedness of all things. Whether through science, art, or spirituality, this contemplation can lead to a more profound sense of wonder, gratitude, and connection to the universe.

1.1 The Natural World as a Reflection of the Divine

The intricate patterns in nature—such as the branching of trees, the spirals of galaxies, or the symmetrical structure of snowflakes—can evoke a profound sense of awe and wonder. Many see these patterns as evidence of a divine intelligence or order underlying the universe. The cycles of the seasons, the phases of the moon, and the ebb and flow of tides can be seen as expressions of a cosmic harmony. These rhythms often inspire spiritual reflection on the cyclical nature of life, death, and rebirth. The web of life, where every organism is connected to others in an intricate balance, can be interpreted as a manifestation of divine unity. This idea is central to many indigenous spiritual traditions and modern ecological thought.

1.2 Sacred Geometry and Architecture

Throughout history, humans have used geometric patterns—such as the golden ratio, mandalas, or the Flower of Life—to represent the divine. These shapes are often seen as universal symbols of harmony and perfection. Many religious structures are designed with intentional patterns and proportions that reflect cosmic order. For example, Gothic cathedrals often use light and geometry to create a sense of transcendence, while Hindu temples are designed to mirror the cosmos. The five Platonic solids (tetrahedron, cube, octahedron, dodecahedron, and icosahedron) are often associated with the classical elements (earth, fire, air, water, and ether) and are found in nature, as well as used in various spiritual practices.

1.3 Mathematics and the Divine

Ancient Greek philosopher Pythagoras (570–495 BCE) believed that mathematics was the language of the divine. The precision and predictability of mathematical laws can be seen as evidence of a higher order. Even in seemingly chaotic systems, such as weather patterns or the stock market, there are underlying patterns and laws. This interplay between chaos and order can inspire contemplation of the divine as both immanent (within the world) and transcendent (beyond it).

1.4 Art and Creativity as Divine Expression

Many artists, from Islamic calligraphers to Renaissance painters, have used patterns to express spiritual themes. The repetition of shapes, colours, and forms can evoke a sense of the infinite and the eternal. The mathematical relationships in music, such as the harmonic series or the structure of a fugue, have long been associated with divine order. Music can be a powerful medium for experiencing the sacred.

1.5 Human Consciousness for the Search for Meaning

Humans are naturally inclined to seek patterns, even in seemingly random events. This tendency can be seen as a spiritual impulse—a desire to find meaning and purpose in the world. Myths and symbols often use patterns to convey more profound truths about the human condition and the nature of the divine. For example, the hero's journey, the cycle of death and rebirth, and the struggle between order and chaos are recurring themes in many spiritual traditions. The patterns of the world are not separate from the divine but are manifestations of it.

In the intricate patterns of nature, in the symmetry of a snowflake, the spiral of a galaxy, or the rhythm of the seasons, we glimpse the divine hand—a cosmic artist weaving order into chaos, beauty into form, and meaning into existence. To see the divine is to recognise the sacred geometry of the universe, where every line, curve, and cycle is a whisper of eternity.

2. What Do We See?

The word *'phenomena'* refers to observable events or occurrences, from the subtle bloom of a flower at dawn to the cataclysmic roar of a distant supernova. Phenomena can be gentle or violent, everyday or rare, ordered as the migration of birds or chaotic as the play of lightning across a storm-wracked sky. Nature offers us an endless parade of such moments—each radiant with its own unique beauty, each hinting at forces and intentions beyond its surface.

But what does it mean to see God in these phenomena? Is it a matter of faith, of interpretation, of pattern-seeking? Or is it something more—a recognition that the very act of perceiving beauty, unity, and meaning in the world is itself a spark of the divine within us? To *"see God in the phenomena"* means recognising the divine presence and attributes within the world around us, both in its grandest scale and its smallest details. The intricate laws governing the universe, the movements of celestial bodies, and the delicate balance of ecosystems can be perceived as reflections of God's immeasurable wisdom and power. Qualities such as love, wisdom, justice, mercy, and goodness, often attributed to God, can be observed in various aspects of creation and human behaviour.

2.1 Immanence of the Divine

Immanence invites us to see the sacred in the ordinary and to recognise the divine as the very essence of existence. The *God in Everything* view holds that God is not distant or removed from the world but is present within it. Every aspect of creation—whether a blooming flower, a thunderstorm, or a human act of kindness—can be seen as a manifestation of the divine. The immanence of God means that every moment is holy, every place is sacred, and every being reflects the divine. Seeing God in the phenomena means recognising the holy in the everyday. It is about finding holiness in the mundane, whether in the laughter of a child, the rustling of leaves, or the vastness of the night sky. Shri Ramakrishna Paramhansa (1836–1886) said, "*The whole universe is the manifestation of God. To see the divine in everything is to see the truth.*"

2.2 Interconnectedness

To see God in the phenomena is to perceive the interconnectedness of all life. American astrophysicist Neil deGrasse Tyson (b. 1958) says candidly, "*We are all connected; to each other, biologically. To the Earth, chemically. To the rest of the universe, atomically.*" The understanding is that everything is part of a greater whole, and that the divine is the unifying force that binds the cosmos together. To see God in the phenomena is to cultivate a profound sense of reverence, wonder, and connection to the world. It is about recognising that the divine is not confined to temples, scriptures, or rituals but is alive and present in every moment, every being, and every aspect of existence. This perspective can transform the way we relate to the world, inspiring us to live with greater awareness, compassion, and gratitude. We are all threads in the same tapestry, waves in the same ocean, leaves on the same tree.

3. Historical Perspectives

Across cultures and epochs, the idea of seeing the divine in the world's phenomena has taken many forms. Ancient Indians saw Brahman as the all-pervading reality. The infinite, eternal, and unchanging Brahman underlies all existence—the substratum of the universe. The *Mahavakya* (great saying) "Tat Tvam Asi" emphasises the unity of the individual self (*Ātman*) with Brahman. It suggests that the divine essence is not separate from us but is our very nature. The phrase *"Sarvam Khalvidam Brahman"* (*All this is Brahman*) from the *Mundaka Upanishad* affirms that everything in the universe is a manifestation of Brahman. The material world, the mind, and even the gods are expressions of this ultimate reality. The entire creation is imbued with the sacred; the divine is not merely behind the curtain, but is the curtain, the stage, and the play.

For the ancient Greeks, divinity was manifest in unpredictability and power—the gods were in the thunder, in the ocean's rage, in the harvest's bounty. Zeus was the god of the sky and thunder. Poseidon ruled the seas and earthquakes. Demeter was the goddess of agriculture and the harvest. Gaia was the primordial goddess of the Earth itself. The Greeks believed that the natural world was imbued with divine presence. Rivers, mountains, trees, and even the wind were seen as inhabited by gods or spirits (nymphs, dryads, etc.). For example, the river god Achelous and the mountain god Ourea were worshipped as divine beings. The Greeks often attributed divine agency to natural elements, believing that the world was alive with divine forces. This animistic view meant that the divine was not separate from the world but was intimately connected to it.

The Jewish tradition, too, is rich in the idea that the wonders of creation are 'the handwriting of God'; each sunrise is a reminder of divine faithfulness. The Torah begins with the account of creation in Genesis, where God speaks the world into existence. This narrative emphasises that the universe is not a random occurrence but the deliberate act of a divine Creator. *"The heavens declare the glory of God; the skies proclaim the work of His hands."* (Psalm 19:1)

Christian mystics, such as the German theologian and mystic Meister Eckhart (1260–1328) and Spanish mystic Teresa of Ávila

(1515–1582), spoke of *"finding God in all things."* Meister Eckhart taught that God is not a distant, external being but the very ground of all existence, present in every aspect of creation and within the soul itself. Through practices of detachment, stillness, and inner awareness, we can realise our oneness with the divine and experience the presence of God in everything. Saint Teresa believed that God can be found in the ordinary activities of daily life, as well as in the simple acts of cooking, cleaning, and caring for others. She taught that prayer is not just a formal practice but a continuous conversation with God.

Persian theologian Imam Ghazali (1058–1111) viewed every phenomenon as a sign pointing to the oneness of God. "The heavens and the earth are filled with signs for those who reflect," he said. By contemplating the natural world, one could come to a deeper understanding of God's wisdom, power, and mercy. Imam Ghazali emphasised the importance of purifying the heart through acts of worship, self-discipline, and remembrance of God. Only a pure heart can truly perceive God's presence in everything.

In more modern times, the scientific revolution shifted attention from mythic interpretation to empirical observation—but even here, many have found the fingerprints of the divine. Isaac Newton (1643–1727), though a scientist par excellence, saw his discoveries as revealing the orderliness of God's laws. Albert Einstein, though not conventionally religious, famously spoke of "spirit manifest in the laws of the universe." Francis Collins (b. 1950) wrote about his DNA discovery in a book titled *The Language of God*: "Freeing God from the burden of special acts of creation does not remove Him as the source of the things that make humanity special, and of the universe itself. It merely shows us something of how He operates."

4. Science and the Sacred

At first glance, the scientific and religious views of the world appear to be in tension. Science seeks natural explanations, while religion often invokes the supernatural. Yet many find in the intricate laws of physics, the elegance of mathematical relationships, and the emergence of consciousness a profound sense of awe—one that borders on the religious. Srinivasa Ramanujan (1887–1920), known for his extraordinary intuition and almost mystical approach to mathematics, attributed his discoveries to divine inspiration. He believed that his mathematical insights were revealed to him by the goddess Namagiri, a form of the Hindu goddess Lakshmi, whom he worshipped.

4.1 Science as a Path to Understanding the Sacred

Science can reveal the awe-inspiring complexity and beauty of the universe, inspiring a sense of wonder and reverence. For many, the discoveries of science—such as the vastness of the cosmos, the intricacy of DNA, or the laws of physics—are seen as glimpses into the sacred. Einstein often spoke of a *"cosmic religious feeling"* that arose from his study of the universe. He viewed science as a means of understanding the divine order underlying the natural world. He said, *"The more I study science, the more I believe in God."*

4.2 The Sacred as a Source of Meaning and Purpose

While science explains the *"how"* of the universe, the sacred often addresses the *"why."* Questions of meaning, purpose, and morality are central to the sacred and can provide a framework for understanding our place in the cosmos. Science can tell us how to clone a human being, but it cannot tell us whether we should. The sacred, through religious and spiritual traditions, offers guidance on these more profound questions. The idea that the soul is not where it lives, but where it loves, highlights the sacred dimension of human experience that transcends the material world. Einstein said, "*Science without religion is lame, religion without science is blind.*"

4.3 The Sacred in the Cosmos

Many religious traditions see the universe as a sacred creation, imbued with divine purpose. Science, by revealing the vastness and complexity of the cosmos, can deepen our sense of awe and wonder at the sacredness of creation. "*We are stardust*" is a scientific fact—that the elements in our bodies were forged in the hearts of stars—yet it can be seen as a sacred connection to the cosmos. We are made of the same stuff as the universe, a concept that resonates with many spiritual traditions. Carl Sagan wrote: "*Science is not only compatible with spirituality; it is a profound source of spirituality.*" Experiencing the sheer immensity of the cosmos or the profound complexity of life on Earth can evoke a sense of awe and wonder, prompting a recognition of a greater force behind creation.

To see God in phenomena, then, is not to see magic or miracles that break the laws of nature, but rather to see in the laws themselves—so reliable yet so mysterious—a hint of intentionality, of purpose, of grace. A sense of interconnectedness with all of existence, an awareness that everything is part of a larger whole, can point to the omnipresent nature of the divine.

5. Phenomena as Parable

Many traditions use the phenomena of the world as parables—teaching stories written not in words, but in wind and water, seed and star. The biblical parables of Jesus often drew upon the natural world, such as the mustard seed, the lilies of the field, and the lost sheep. These stories invite us to see in the everyday not just a backdrop, but a message. Likewise, Buddhist teachings highlight impermanence by observing the falling of autumn leaves or the rising and passing of clouds, reminding us to live with awareness and compassion. The Indigenous peoples of many lands have long regarded the land, animals, and rivers as kin, imbued with spirit and wisdom.

5.1 Symbolism in Nature

The changing seasons—spring, summer, autumn, and winter—are often seen as parables for the cycles of life, death, and rebirth. In many spiritual traditions, these natural phenomena symbolise the eternal rhythms of existence. The biblical passage, *"For everything there is a season, and a time for every matter under heaven"* (Ecclesiastes 3:1), reflects the idea that the cycles of nature are a metaphor for the rhythms of human life. The growth of a seed into a plant is a familiar parable for spiritual growth and transformation. In the New Testament, Jesus uses the mustard seed as a metaphor for the kingdom of God:

"The kingdom of heaven is like a mustard seed, which a man took and planted in his field. Though it is the smallest of all seeds, yet when it grows, it is the largest of garden plants." (Matthew 13:31-32)

5.2 Phenomena as Mystical Symbols

In many spiritual traditions, light and darkness are used as parables for the struggle between good and evil, or the journey from ignorance to enlightenment. The biblical verse, *"The light shines in the darkness, and the darkness has not overcome it"* (John 1:5), uses the image of light as a metaphor for the triumph of divine truth over ignorance and evil.

In Buddhism, the lotus flower is a powerful symbol of spiritual awakening. The lotus grows in muddy water but blooms into a beautiful flower, symbolising the potential for enlightenment even while suffering. *"Just as a lotus flower grows out of the mud and blossoms into a beautiful flower, so too can the human soul rise above the challenges of life and achieve enlightenment."* This teaching uses the lotus flower as a parable for the spiritual journey.

5.3 Dattatreya's 24 Gurus

Dattatreya is a revered figure in Hinduism. In the *Shrimad Bhagavatam*, Dattatreya explains that he learned spiritual lessons from the 24 elements of nature and living beings, each of which served as a teacher in his journey toward enlightenment. This teaching emphasises that wisdom can be found everywhere in nature if one is attentive and humble enough to learn.

From the earth, which bears the weight of all living beings without complaint, Dattatreya learned the importance of patience, endurance, and remaining unshaken in the face of adversity. The moon waxes and wanes cyclically, teaching that life is full of cycles—joy and sorrow, success and failure—and that one should remain equanimous through these changes. From the spider, which weaves its web and later withdraws it, Dattatreya learned that the universe is created and dissolved by the divine, just as the spider creates and withdraws its web.

6. Personal Experience of the Divine

For many, the sense of seeing God in the phenomena is deeply personal, even wordless. It may come in a shaft of sunlight through old stained glass, in the hush before dawn in the forest, in the intricate patterns of frost on a winter window. Such moments are often marked not by certainty, but by wonder—a *"heart-leap"*, a sudden swelling of gratitude or reverence.

According to Australian neurophysiologist John Eccles (1903–1997), who won the 1963 Nobel Prize in Physiology or Medicine, *"If I consider reality as I experience it, the primary experience I have is of my own existence as a self-conscious being, which I believe is God-created."*

This is not to say that every sunset or every rhythm of the tides reveals the divine directly, or in the same way to each observer. The experience is shaped by culture, upbringing, disposition, and the questions one brings to the world. For one, the migration of geese may be a natural occurrence; for another, it is a rich metaphor for life, community, resilience, and purpose. Their V-formation flight, shared leadership, and seasonal journeys offer profound lessons about teamwork, adaptability, and the cycles of life. By observing the geese, we can learn to navigate our journeys with grace, purpose, and a sense of connection to the world around us. Their flight across the sky is a reminder that we are all part of a larger journey, guided by the unseen forces of nature and the universe.

In truth, the personal experience of the divine cannot be taught or replicated—it must be encountered. It often arises in stillness, when the noise of daily life subsides and the mind becomes receptive to subtler dimensions of being. In that silence, one senses that existence itself is sacred, that every breath participates in a rhythm older than time. These moments are not escapes from reality, but deeper immersions into it—a recognition that the sacred is woven through the very fabric of the ordinary.

Such experiences may also grow through acts of love, service, and creativity. When we give selflessly, create beauty, or forgive sincerely, we momentarily transcend the confines of ego and glimpse the divine impulse that animates all life. The personal experience of God, then, is not confined to revelation or ritual—it unfolds through awareness, compassion, and participation in the mystery of being. Each of us, in our own way, becomes a living vessel through which the divine continues its expression in the world.

As Gurdev Rabindranath Tagore wrote, "The same stream of life that runs through my veins night and day runs through the world and dances in rhythmic measures."

7. Living in Wonder

Much depends upon how one conceives of God. Some traditions speak of God as wholly transcendent, beyond the world and its phenomena; others emphasise immanence, the presence of the divine in and through all things. The divine is not separate from creation but is its very life and energy.

Jesus says in The Gospel of Thomas (non-canonical), "The kingdom of God is within you, and all around you. It is not in buildings of wood and stone. Split a piece of wood, and I am there. Lift a stone, and you will find me."

Crucially, to see God in the phenomena is not merely a matter of observation, but of interpretation and response. It is to allow the world's beauty and terror, its order and chaos, to speak to the deepest parts of ourselves. How we respond to suffering, to joy, to the intricacy of a spider's web or the thunderous might of a waterfall shapes not only our sense of the divine but also our actions in the world.

The divine is not found in the heavens, but in the here and now. It is in the ordinary, the everyday, the mundane. To see God is to see the sacred in the simple. This encounter can inspire gratitude, stewardship, and compassion. If the world is a sacred gift, then caring for it is a form of worship. If every being bears the mark of the divine, then reverence extends to all—to people, to animals, to the Earth itself.

Of course, the phenomena of the world are not always beautiful or comforting. Natural disasters, disease, and suffering raise hard questions—sometimes called *"the problem of evil"*—that challenge easy theological answers. Can we see God in the storm, in the earthquake, or in the silence that follows tragedy? Some traditions respond with faith in God's ultimate goodness, while others offer the assurance that meaning exists even in suffering. Still others find divinity not in the events themselves, but in the human capacity to respond with courage, kindness, and resilience.

To live in wonder is to stand before existence with open eyes and an open heart—to see not just what is, but what is possible. It is the posture of awe that transforms knowledge into wisdom and observation into reverence. Wonder bridges science and spirituality, inviting us to explore without arrogance and to question without losing faith. In wonder, the mind bows before the mystery of being, and the soul finds renewal in curiosity. When we cultivate this sense of sacred wonder, every breath becomes a prayer, every act of care a hymn, and every moment—however ordinary—a revelation of the divine presence.

8. Summary

To see God in the phenomena is to live attentively, with eyes open to the marvels and mysteries that surround us. It is to cultivate a posture of wonder—neither naïve nor cynical, but willing to receive the world as a gift, as a mystery, as an invitation. Whether through the lens of faith or science, whether in moments of silence or song, the phenomena of the world invite us into deeper reflection.

Beneath the surface of things, we may glimpse a pattern, a presence, a whisper of the divine. In the flicker of a flame, in the rush of the river, in the gaze of another, the possibility remains: that God is not far, but near—woven through the phenomena of the world, waiting to be seen.

7

Feeling God Within

"God illumines the mind and shines within it. One cannot know God through the mind. One can but turn the mind inwards and merge it in God."

—Ramana Maharshi
Hindu sage (1879–1950)

1. Understanding the Inner Experience

To feel God within is to embark upon a journey both intimate and infinite—a pilgrimage not to distant shrines or sacred mountains, but to the quiet, uncharted landscapes of one's own heart. Across centuries and cultures, seekers have spoken of an enigmatic, transformative presence: a light that glows behind the veil of thought, a voice that whispers in moments of silence, a pulse that beats beneath our every joy and sorrow. What does it mean to feel God within, and how do we cultivate this sense of divine presence amid the everyday?

The sensation of God's presence is often described as an ineffable knowing—a certainty that neither logic nor language can fully capture. For some, it arrives as a gentle warmth or a sense of peace that washes over them during meditation or prayer. For others, it is a sudden, overwhelming awe while witnessing the beauty of nature, the innocence of a child, or the vastness of the night sky. It may be a profound sense of belonging, acceptance, or love that seems to emanate not from external circumstances, but from the very core of one's being.

In mystical traditions, this experience is termed "*immanence*"—the belief that the divine is not solely transcendent and far off, but indwelling, closer to us than our breath. The divine is not separate from the world but is actively involved in its creation, maintenance, and dissolution. Sufi poet Rumi wrote, "*I searched for God and found only myself. I searched for myself and found only God.*" Likewise, Christian mystics such as Teresa of Ávila and John of the Cross (1542–1591) spoke of an "*inner castle*" or a "*dark night of the soul,*" where God is encountered in the depths of the self.

The immanence of God is a core concept in Indian philosophical and religious thought, particularly within Hinduism. It signifies that God is not just transcendent (existing beyond the material world) but also immanent (present within the material world and all beings). Ancient Hindu scriptures, such as the Vedas, Upanishads, and the *Bhagavad Gita*, affirm God's immanence. God is both beyond the universe and also pervades it, residing within all things. Swami Vivekananda said, "*All that is real in me is God; all that is real in God is I. The gulf between God and me is thus bridged. Thus, by knowing God, we find that the kingdom of heaven is within us.*"

2. Internal Psychic Organs

In various philosophical and spiritual traditions, the term "*internal psychic organs*" often refers to the mind, intellect, consciousness, and ego, collectively known as *Antaḥkaraṇa*. These are considered the inner instruments or faculties through which we perceive, process information, and experience the world. While not physical organs in the biological sense, they are understood as the non-physical components that shape our subjective reality and play a crucial role in our thoughts, feelings, and actions.

2.1 Mind *(Manas)*

Manas is often described as the "thinking mind" or the mind responsible for processing sensory input, emotions, and thoughts. It is the faculty that collects impressions from the senses (*Indriyas*) like seeing, hearing, touching, tasting, and smelling. It acts as a bridge or mediator between the external senses and the higher mental faculties of *Buddhi* (intellect) and *Ahamkara* (ego).

2.2 Intellect *(Buddhi)*

The intellect is associated with reason, judgement, and decision-making. It analyses information received by the mind and helps in forming judgements. *Samyak buddhi* (right intellect) is that which shows things as they are.

2.3 Ego *(Ahamkara)*

The ego is the sense of "I-ness" or individuality. It is the part of us that identifies with our experiences and creates a sense of self. It separates the individual from the universal self. In some philosophical writings, *Ahamkara* is compared to wish-granting but deceptive forces, often twisting desires and leading to negative consequences.

2.4 Consciousness *(Chitta)*

Consciousness is the fundamental awareness or sentience that underlies all mental processes. It is the ground of being from which all other psychic functions arise. An Indian proverb says, *"Chitta is a blank canvas, and your actions, thoughts, and emotions paint on it."*

These internal psychic organs are not isolated entities but interconnected aspects of our inner landscape. For example, the mind receives sensory input, the intellect analyses it, the ego identifies with the experience, and consciousness provides the backdrop for it all.

Some traditions also include the concept of the *Psychic Being* (*Chaitanya*). It refers to a pure consciousness that is aware of itself and of others. This deeper, more subtle aspect of the self is often associated with the soul or spirit, believed to be the source of our intuition, higher wisdom, and spiritual aspiration.

3. The Universality of the Experience

Despite differences in theology and practice, people from diverse backgrounds report similar sensations of the sacred within. In Hindu philosophy, the *Atman* and *Paramatman* represent the individual soul and the Supreme Soul, respectively. The *Atman* is considered a spark of the divine, an eternal and conscious entity within each living being, while the *Paramatman* is the all-pervading, universal consciousness that is the source of all existence.

Their relationship is often described through analogies:

Two birds on a tree: one (*Atman*) eats the fruits (worldly experiences), while the other (*Paramatman*) observes.

The Sun and its rays: the rays (*Atman*) are part of the Sun (*Paramatman*), yet appear separate.

Spark and fire: the spark (*Atman*) is part of the great fire (*Paramatman*).

Buddhism, though non-theistic, also points to an inner awakening—*Nirvana* in Theravada, *Bodhi* in Mahayana—a liberation from suffering and rebirth (*Samsara*). This realisation transcends dualistic perception, leading to a profound understanding of reality.

Modern contemplative practices, such as mindfulness meditation and centring prayer, provide accessible pathways to this sense of inner divinity. Even secular meditation offers moments of clarity, peace, or empathy that feel transcendent—removing religious language or ritual but retaining attentiveness to the sacred within.

4. Recognising the Signs

How does one know they are feeling God within? The signs vary, yet common themes include:

4.1 Peace Beyond Understanding

A calm that persists regardless of external chaos: *"And the peace of God, which transcends all understanding, will guard your hearts and your minds in Christ Jesus."* (Philippians 4:7)

4.2 Unconditional Love

A sense of being loved and of loving others without judgment or reservation. *"Love is that condition in which the happiness of another person is essential to your own."* (Anonymous)

4.3 Guidance and Wisdom

Insights or intuitions that appear in surrender rather than striving. Anne Morrow Lindbergh wrote: *"If you surrender completely to the moments as they pass, you live more richly those moments."*

4.4 Compassion and Empathy

A natural desire to help, motivated by kinship. Dietrich Bonhoeffer said: *"We must learn to regard people less in the light of what they do or omit to do, and more in the light of what they suffer."*

4.5 Awe and Reverence

Wonder at life's mysteries, coupled with humility. Tricia Levenseller writes: *"It's not about need; it's* about showing reverence."

5. Obstacles to the Inner Divine

Obstacles arise from ego, attachment, fear, doubt, habits, and trauma, as well as from external pressures—cultural norms, doctrines, and negative influences. Gandhi said: *"I will not let anyone walk through my mind with their dirty feet."*

Overcoming obstacles requires cultivating faith, practising surrender, meditation, courage, and positive habits, along with guidance from teachers or mentors.

6. Practical Ways to Experience God

Meditation and Prayer: "The purpose of prayer is to reveal the presence of God equally present, all the time, in every condition." (Oswald Chambers)

Nature Immersion: "Nature is God's living, visible garment." (Goethe)

6.1 Seva (Selfless Service)

Serving others with no expectation of return fosters inner divinity. Creative Expression: Music, art, writing, or dance become channels of the sacred.

Max Lucado reminds us: *"He is nearer than you think."*

7. The Transformative Impact

Feeling God within nurtures humility, resilience, hope, and compassion. It transforms life into sacred unfolding. Augustine wrote: *"To fall in love with God is the greatest romance; to seek him the greatest adventure; to find him, the greatest human achievement."*

8. God and Science

Far from disproving God, science has deepened awe at the fine-tuned order of the universe, from cosmic laws to cellular intricacy. Ramanujan, Newton, and Einstein all pointed to this sense of divine order.

Even quantum observation shows that matter and energy are influenced by awareness. This affirms the teaching: our lives are shaped by the choices we make.

9. Summary

The journey to feel God within is personal yet universal. Whether described as God, Spirit, Self, or *"the more,"* the inner divine affirms that we are never alone, and that the sacred dwells as close as our beating hearts.

8

Mind as a Portal

"All knowledge that the world has ever received comes from the mind; the infinite library of the universe is in our own mind."

—Swami Vivekananda
(1863–1902)

---

1. Connecting to the Universe

The mind is a tapestry of thoughts, dreams, and perceptions—a marvel of evolution and a gateway to unexplored realms. Throughout history, mystics, philosophers, and scientists have posited that the mind is not merely an organ for rational thought but also a portal to a deeper, universal consciousness. The mind can be seen as both a tool for navigating the material world and a bridge to a more profound, universal awareness. By exploring its depths, one can uncover insights that transcend individual thought and touch the very essence of existence.

In many spiritual traditions, such as Advaita Vedanta, Buddhism, and mysticism, the mind is regarded as a gateway to a higher, universal consciousness. This perspective suggests that through meditation, introspection, or altered states of awareness, one can transcend individual thought and connect with a more expansive, interconnected reality. The personal "self" is seen as a temporary construct, and the true nature of consciousness is universal and boundless. Beyond rational thought, the mind is also the source of intuition, creativity, and inspiration. These faculties often arise from a deeper, less structured level of awareness, suggesting that the mind taps into a wellspring of universal wisdom or collective knowledge.

The concept of "cosmic consciousness" refers to a heightened state of awareness in which an individual experiences a profound sense of unity with the universe, transcending the boundaries of the ego and the individual self. This idea has been explored in various spiritual, philosophical, and mystical traditions, as well as in modern psychology and consciousness studies. It suggests that the mind is capable of accessing a deeper, universal reality that underlies all existence.

Beyond our ordinary, ego-bound awareness lies a deeper, universal reality that we can access through spiritual practice, meditation, or moments of profound insight. Whether viewed through the lens of mysticism, philosophy, or science, cosmic consciousness invites us to explore the interconnectedness of all existence and the limitless nature of the human mind. The experience of cosmic consciousness is profoundly personal and subjective, making it difficult to study or verify scientifically. Not everyone may experience cosmic consciousness, and it is often described as a rare or fleeting state that requires significant spiritual or psychological preparation.

2. Defining Cosmic Consciousness

Cosmic consciousness is a term popularised by Canadian psychiatrist Richard Maurice Bucke (1837–1902) in his book *Cosmic Consciousness: A Study in the Evolution of the Human Mind*. Bucke described it as "a higher form of consciousness than that possessed by the ordinary man." This state is characterised by a sense of unity with the cosmos, boundless love, and a profound understanding of existence.

Other thinkers—ranging from Eastern sages to Western philosophers—have described similar experiences. In Vedantic philosophy, this state is akin to "samadhi", where the individual self merges with the universal Self. In Sufism, it relates to "fana", the dissolution of the ego in the divine. American psychologist Abraham Maslow (1908–1970) explored the concept of "peak experiences", which resonate with cosmic consciousness, describing moments of awe and unity that transcend ordinary perception.

The idea of the mind as a portal implies that consciousness is not bound within the skull but rather a field that can expand beyond the individual. This shifts our perspective from viewing the mind as a closed loop to seeing it as a receiver and transmitter of universal signals. The notion that the mind might be connected to a fundamental field of consciousness that permeates the universe leads to the conclusion that the mind is a portal to a deeper reality.

2.1 Carl Jung

Swiss psychiatrist Carl Jung (1875–1961) introduced the concept of the collective unconscious, a shared reservoir of archetypes and experiences that transcends individual minds. This idea suggests that the mind is not an isolated entity, but instead connected to a broader, shared consciousness. Jung argued that the collective unconscious is inherited, much like physical traits. It is not the result of personal experience but is part of the human species' psychological heritage.

This means that all humans have access to the same archetypes and symbols, which influence our thoughts, behaviours, and creative expressions. Jung believed that dreams are a direct pathway to the collective unconscious. In dreams, archetypes and universal symbols often emerge, providing insight into the deeper layers of the psyche. By analysing dreams, individuals can gain access to the collective unconscious and work towards psychological integration.

2.2 David Bohm

American theoretical physicist David Bohm (1917–1992) introduced the concept of the collective mind as part of his broader exploration of wholeness and interconnectedness in the universe. Bohm's ideas extend beyond physics into philosophy, psychology, and consciousness studies, offering a unique perspective on how individual minds might be part of a larger, collective consciousness. Bohm suggested that consciousness is not merely a by-product of the brain but a fundamental aspect of the universe. He saw the collective mind as a manifestation of this universal consciousness, which underlies all of reality. This view aligns with panpsychism, the philosophical idea that consciousness is a fundamental property of the universe, present in all matter.

3. The Neuroscientific Perspective

Neuroscience has revealed the brain's remarkable plasticity and its ability to generate altered states of consciousness. Studies using fMRI and EEG scans have shown that meditation, deep contemplation, and even moments of creative flow can produce unique brainwave patterns associated with unity and transcendence. The Default Mode Network (DMN), a set of interconnected brain regions, is particularly active during self-referential thinking but quietens during meditative states, correlating with experiences of ego dissolution.

4. The Quantum Brain Hypothesis

Some theorists have speculated that consciousness may be linked to quantum phenomena. English physicist Roger Penrose (b. 1931), who won the 2020 Nobel Prize in Physics, and American anaesthesiologist Stuart Hameroff (b. 1947) have proposed that the brain's microtubules might be sites of quantum processing, potentially enabling connections with a universal "field" of consciousness. Their Orchestrated Objective Reduction (Orch-OR) theory posits that consciousness emerges from quantum processes within the brain. Specifically, they argue that microtubules (structures within neurons) are the site of quantum computations that give rise to conscious experience. This hypothesis suggests that the mind could, under certain circumstances, access realms beyond the ordinary.

4.1 Universal Mathematical Truths

If consciousness is indeed rooted in quantum processes, then the non-local nature of quantum entanglement could imply that minds are not entirely isolated but are part of a larger, interconnected system. The mind is not confined to the physical brain but belongs to a wider, non-algorithmic reality. This could imply a form of collective consciousness that transcends individual, computational minds.

Individual consciousnesses are linked at a quantum level. For example, mathematical truths exist independently of human minds in a timeless, abstract realm. This suggests that human consciousness has access to this realm, allowing us to discover mathematical truths, and that consciousness itself is part of a larger, universal structure.

4.2 Teleology

Derived from the Greek word *telos*, meaning "end" or "purpose", teleology is the philosophical idea that there is an inherent purpose or design in nature and the universe. It suggests that events and processes are directed towards an end goal or final cause.

In a teleological framework, the universe's purpose could be seen as the expression or realisation of universal consciousness. This aligns with the idea that the universe is not random but is designed to bring about conscious beings who can experience and understand it. Whether viewed as a divine purpose, a fundamental aspect of reality, or a guiding force behind evolution, the interplay between teleology and universal consciousness presents a profound and holistic perspective on the universe and our place within it. American philosopher Thomas Nagel (b. 1937) says, "In addition to physical law of the familiar kind, there are other laws of nature that are 'biased toward the marvellous.'"

5. Inseparable From the Universe

Across cultures, spiritual practices have been developed to tune the mind into the cosmic frequency. Meditation, prayer, chanting, and ritual are all methods designed to quieten the mind's chatter and open the inner senses to a deeper reality. In Zen Buddhism, practitioners seek *kensho*—the direct experience of one's true nature, inseparable from the universe. It is considered a preliminary or partial experience of enlightenment (*satori*), which is a deeper and more complete awakening.

Kensho involves a direct, non-conceptual understanding of one's true self, beyond the ego and intellectual constructs. It is a sudden, fleeting experience, though it can have a lasting impact on one's perspective and practice. *Kensho* is typically sought through intensive meditation (*zazen*), *koan* practice, and other Zen disciplines. It is not something that can be achieved solely through intellectual study. While *kensho* is a significant milestone, it is not the ultimate goal in Zen. The full realisation of enlightenment (*satori*) involves a deeper and more continuous state of awakening.

Indigenous shamans often use drumming, dance, and plant medicines to alter perception and commune with the cosmos. Shamanic practices are typically grounded in the belief that all things—humans, animals, plants, and the cosmos—are interconnected. The shaman acts as a mediator between these realms. Shamans see themselves as conduits for cosmic wisdom, accessing knowledge from the spirit world to guide their people.

The Native American Church uses peyote, a cactus containing the psychoactive compound mescaline, in ceremonial contexts to commune with the Great Spirit and seek healing and guidance.

6. Practical Approaches to Accessing Cosmic Consciousness

How does one use the mind as a portal to cosmic awareness? While the process is deeply personal, and each individual's journey is unique, certain practices are widely recognised for fostering the necessary openness and receptivity.

The breath is a bridge between the conscious and subconscious mind. Practices like *pranayama* (yogic breathing) help regulate the nervous system, calm the mind, and facilitate access to expanded states of consciousness. Coupled with *asanas* (physical postures), yoga serves as a holistic discipline for harmonising body, mind, and spirit.

Meditation is the most time-honoured method. By observing one's thoughts without attachment, the meditator gradually detaches from the ego, the sense of a separate, isolated self. Over time, moments of silent clarity arise, wherein the boundaries between self and universe seem to dissolve. Techniques such as Transcendental Meditation, mindfulness, and loving-kindness meditation can all serve as entry points.

6.1 Transcendental Meditation

Developed by Maharishi Mahesh Yogi (1917–2008), Transcendental Meditation (TM) gained widespread popularity in the 1960s. Known for its simplicity and accessibility, it became a popular choice for those seeking stress reduction, mental clarity, and spiritual growth.

TM involves the silent repetition of a mantra—a specific sound or phrase—given to the practitioner by a TM teacher. The mantra is chosen based on the individual and is intended to serve as a vehicle for transcending ordinary thought and accessing deeper levels of consciousness. TM is typically practised for 15–20 minutes, twice a day, once in the morning and once in the evening. The primary goal of TM is to transcend ordinary thought and experience a state of pure consciousness, also known as transcendental awareness.

6.2 Mindfulness

Fully attending to the present moment, noticing sensations, emotions, and thoughts as they arise and pass. Mindfulness encourages practitioners to focus on the present moment, letting go of past regrets and future anxieties. By observing thoughts, emotions, and sensations without judgment, mindfulness allows practitioners to detach from the ego and experience a more expansive awareness.

This heightened awareness can lead to a sense of timelessness, where the boundaries between past, present, and future dissolve. As mindfulness deepens, practitioners may experience moments of expansion, where the sense of self extends beyond the individual body and mind, leading to a feeling of oneness with the universe.

6.3 Loving-Kindness

Cultivating goodwill, compassion, and unity towards oneself and all beings. While it is often used to develop emotional well-being and empathy, it can also be a powerful tool for accessing cosmic consciousness—a state of profound interconnectedness and unity with all beings and the universe.

In deep states of loving-kindness meditation, practitioners may experience pure love and bliss, which are often described as qualities of cosmic consciousness. These states can be profoundly transformative, leading to a lasting sense of unity with the cosmos. Loving-kindness meditation can help practitioners transcend dualistic thinking (self vs other, good vs bad) and access a state of non-dual awareness, where all distinctions dissolve, leaving only pure consciousness.

7. The Experience of Cosmic Consciousness

The experience of cosmic consciousness is a profound, transformative state of awareness characterised by a sense of unity with the universe, timelessness, expanded awareness, bliss, and wisdom. It can be accessed through meditation, spiritual awakening, connection with nature, or psychedelic experiences.

Rooted in both ancient spiritual traditions and modern interpretations, cosmic consciousness provides a profound insight into the interconnectedness of all life and the ultimate reality that underlies existence. Whether experienced suddenly or developed over time, cosmic consciousness is a gateway to transcendence and the realisation of oneness with the cosmos.

7.1 Unity and Oneness

One of the most common experiences in cosmic consciousness is the dissolution of the ego—the sense of a separate self. The individual feels a profound unity with all beings, nature, and the universe itself. There is a deep realisation that all things are interconnected and part of a single, unified whole. This can lead to a sense of universal love and compassion for all life.

Ralph Waldo Emerson (1803–1882) explained, *"The Oversoul is that great nature in which we rest, as the earth lies in the soft arms of the atmosphere; that Unity, that Over-soul, within which every man's particular being is contained and made one with all other."*

7.2 Timelessness and Eternity

In cosmic consciousness, the experience of time often changes or disappears altogether. The individual may feel as though they are existing in an eternal present, where past, present, and future merge into a single continuum. This state is often described as the eternal now, where the individual is fully present and aware, free from the constraints of linear time.

Sri Aurobindo said, "*Cosmic consciousness is the realisation of the infinite, the eternal, and the universal in and through the individual self.*"

7.3 Expanded Awareness

The individual may experience a sense of vastness or infinite space, where the boundaries of the physical body and mind seem to dissolve. This can lead to a feeling of being one with the cosmos. Some people describe accessing higher dimensions of reality, where they perceive the universe in a more complex, multi-layered way.

Carl Jung said, "*The self is not only the centre but also the whole circumference which embraces both conscious and unconscious; it is the centre of this totality, just as the ego is the centre of the conscious mind.*"

These experiences can arise spontaneously or as the culmination of long practice. While transformative, they may also be fleeting. The challenge is to integrate insights into daily life, allowing them to inform actions, attitudes, and relationships.

Cosmic consciousness often brings with it a profound moral and ethical awakening. When one perceives the unity of all existence, the impulse to harm, exploit, or dominate naturally diminishes. Compassion and responsibility arise not as commandments but as spontaneous expressions of understanding. In recognising the sacredness of all life, the individual begins to act as a custodian of harmony—treating people, animals, and the Earth with reverence. Such consciousness does not withdraw from the world; it participates in it with deeper empathy and purpose.

Moreover, the experience invites humility. To touch the infinite is to realise the limits of one's own knowing and the vastness of the mystery that remains. Cosmic consciousness, therefore, is not an end state but a beginning—a call to live wisely, creatively, and lovingly within the web of existence. As the mystic Pierre Teilhard de Chardin wrote, "We are not human beings having a spiritual experience; we are spiritual beings having a human experience."

8. Integrating Cosmic Consciousness into Daily Living

Accessing cosmic consciousness is not an escape from life's challenges but an invitation to live more deeply engaged. The wisdom gained from such experiences can foster compassion, resilience, and ethical action. Relationships become opportunities for genuine connection, work is imbued with meaning, and adversity is faced with equanimity.

8.1 Cultivate Mindfulness and Presence

Bring mindfulness to everyday activities, such as eating, walking, or even washing dishes. Focus on the present moment, noticing the sensations, thoughts, and emotions that arise. This helps you stay connected to the eternal now, a key aspect of cosmic consciousness.

Use your breath as an anchor to the present moment. Take a few deep breaths throughout the day to reconnect with the universal flow of life. Take short pauses during the day to step back from busyness and reconnect with a sense of expanded awareness. Ask yourself, *"How can I bring a sense of unity and interconnectedness into this moment?"*

German teacher and author Eckhart Tolle (b. 1948) says, *"Realise deeply that the present moment is all you ever have. Make the Now the primary focus of your life."*

8.2 Live with Compassion and Loving-Kindness

Regularly practise loving-kindness meditation, extending feelings of love and compassion to yourself, loved ones, strangers, and even those you find difficult. This helps you embody the universal love experienced in cosmic consciousness.

Perform small acts of kindness throughout the day, such as assisting a stranger in need, offering a smile, or listening deeply to someone. These actions reinforce the sense of interconnectedness with all beings.

When interacting with others, practise deep listening—listening without judgement or the need to respond. This fosters a sense of unity and empathy.

Cultivate gratitude for the simple things in life—a warm cup of tea, the beauty of nature, or the presence of loved ones. Gratitude helps you stay connected to the abundance and interconnectedness of the universe.

Thich Nhat Hanh says, "Walk as if you are kissing the Earth with your feet. Every step is a moment of connection with the cosmos."

8.3 Embrace Non-Duality in Daily Life

In moments of conflict or challenge, remind yourself that all opposites are part of a unified whole. For example, when faced with difficulty, see it as an opportunity for growth and transformation rather than something to resist.

Practise non-judgement towards yourself and others. Recognise that everyone is on their own journey, and all experiences are part of the cosmic dance.

Embrace the impermanence of life, knowing that all things—both joyful and painful—are temporary. This helps you stay grounded in the eternal now. Rumi said, "*You are not a drop in the ocean. You are the entire ocean in a drop.*"

While the pursuit of cosmic consciousness can be enriching, it is not without hazards. Some may become enamoured with altered states to the detriment of practical life, or fall prey to spiritual bypassing—using lofty experiences to avoid confronting personal issues. Discernment, grounding practices, and the guidance of experienced mentors are essential for a balanced journey. In the words of the poet William Blake, "*If the doors of perception were cleansed, everything would appear to man as it is: Infinite.*"

May your journey through the mind's portal lead you to ever-widening circles of awareness, wonder, and unity with the cosmos.

To live with cosmic consciousness is to recognise that the universe is not something outside of us—it is within us, breathing through our thoughts, actions, and relationships. The stars that shine above are the same elements that pulse in our veins; the vastness of the cosmos mirrors the vastness of our inner world. When we awaken to this truth, daily life becomes a sacred expression of the infinite. Every word we speak, every gesture we make, carries the vibration of creation itself. Cosmic consciousness thus transforms ordinary existence into a living meditation, reminding us that we are not mere observers of the universe, but conscious participants in its unfolding harmony.

9. Summary

The mind, far from being a mere vessel of thoughts, is a luminous gateway to the vastness of existence. Approached with reverence, discipline, and curiosity, it can reveal the interconnectedness at the heart of reality. By employing meditation, breathwork, contemplation, creative expression, and communion with nature, one may glimpse cosmic consciousness and, in doing so, realise that the universe itself is not something we observe from afar, but a living presence within which we eternally belong.

As Carl Sagan beautifully said, "We are a way for the cosmos to know itself." In awakening to this truth, we become both the observer and the observed—an inseparable part of the grand unfolding of creation.

9

The Ultimate Experience

"We can never obtain peace in the outer world until we make peace with ourselves."

—Dalai Lama XIV

The Head of the Tibetan People (b. 1935)

1. An Exploration of the Human Spirit

A state of contentment and emotional well-being, including joy, happiness, and bliss, is celebrated as the ultimate human experience. Although it is felt by all, albeit for short periods, it remains misunderstood and often eludes comprehension. Some see it as a condition of intentional psychological or spiritual calmness sustained in the face of pressures, which is what we mean when we talk about having inner peace, or peace of mind. Others refer to it as a state in which one's mind operates at peak efficiency, regardless of external factors. Scientists call it a state of psychological *homeostasis*—the polar opposite of stress and anxiety.

When one's mental state is unaffected by stress, we say that they are peaceful, tranquil, and serene. Breathing exercises, prayer, meditation, tai chi, and yoga are some of the cultural practices that may lead to a condition of inner calm. An encounter with self-awareness is a common metaphor for this state of tranquillity in spiritual traditions, where inner peace is understood as an interconnected state of being characterised by calmness, contentment, and freedom from mental distress, achieved through acceptance, mindfulness, and a balanced approach to life's challenges.

It is not easy to define inner peace, but it is often seen as an effect that can be achieved through five pathways.

1.1 Connection with the Divine

Many spiritual traditions view tranquillity as a result of a deep connection with a higher power, the universe, or one's true inner self, providing purpose and reassurance. American author Marianne Williamson (b. 1952) uses the metaphor of lamps plugged into the "electricity of God" to describe connecting with the divine through prayer, forgiveness, meditation, and love. She states that the more people who "plug in", the more darkness will be removed from the world.

1.2 Through Practices

Spiritual practices such as meditation, prayer, and mindfulness are central to achieving inner peace by quietening the mind and focusing on the present moment. According to French priest Pierre Teilhard de Chardin (1881–1955), *"We are not human beings having a spiritual experience; we are spiritual beings having a human experience."*

1.3 Release of Attachments

A core element of spiritual tranquillity involves letting go of attachments to material possessions, desires, and ego-driven pursuits, leading to a sense of freedom. You can only lose what you cling to. Suffering often stems from attachment to things, people, outcomes, or even ideas that are inherently temporary. Pain and disappointment are inevitable when clinging tightly to transient things that change or are lost.

1.4 Alignment with Values

Living in accordance with one's core spiritual values and beliefs fosters a greater sense of inner peace and harmony. *Live your life in such a way that those who know you but don't know God will come to know God because they know you.* Carl Jung said, "*The privilege of a lifetime is to become who you really are.*"

1.5 Ethical Living

Many spiritual perspectives emphasise that an ethical life, defined by virtues and principles, is a prerequisite for experiencing true tranquillity. *Live so that when your children think of fairness and integrity, they think of you.* Contemporary American media personality Gerard Braud says, "*Ethical behaviour is doing in private what you would do if the world were watching.*"

In the ceaseless rhythm of modern life, where obligations and aspirations blend into a cacophony of tasks and distractions, the promise of inner peace gleams like a distant oasis. While achievements, possessions, and even relationships might offer fleeting moments of joy, it is the steady flame of tranquillity within that sustains true fulfilment. Inner peace is not merely a passive state or a retreat from life's turbulence; rather, it is the ultimate experience—a profound alignment of mind, body, and spirit that endures regardless of external circumstance.

2. The Nature of Inner Peace

To truly understand why inner peace stands as the pinnacle of human aspiration, one must first grasp its nature. Inner peace is a sense of calm, acceptance, and contentment that comes from within, independent of the world outside. It is not an escape from reality, but a way of being in the world with equanimity. This serenity springs from self-awareness, compassion, and the ability to remain centred even amid chaos.

Contrary to common belief, inner peace is not synonymous with inactivity, nor does it require withdrawal from responsibilities or ambitions. Instead, it is the foundation upon which clarity, resilience, and creativity are built. When the mind ceases its relentless pursuit of validation or fear, one is free to act purposefully and joyfully, embracing the fullness of existence.

2.1 Emotional Regulation and Self-Awareness

It involves managing one's thoughts and emotions effectively, understanding reactions to various situations, and finding balance even in the face of adversity.

2.2 Acceptance

This encompasses accepting oneself, others, and past experiences without judgement, and letting go of worries about the future.

2.3 Contentment and Appreciation

A key indicator of inner peace is finding joy in the present moment and developing a profound sense of appreciation for what one has, rather than dwelling on what is lacking.

2.4 Harmony and Connectedness

Inner peace also fosters a sense of connection with others and with nature, promoting an inner feeling of belonging and peace.

2.5 Resilience

Individuals experiencing inner peace are more adept at handling stress and mental challenges with greater control.

3. Why Inner Peace Surpasses External Success

The world often equates happiness with tangible accomplishments, such as prestigious careers, financial security, or social recognition. Yet, history and personal experience reveal that external gains, however gratifying, are transient. The thrill of acquisition soon fades, and anxieties, insecurities, or new desires arise to take their place. Without inner peace, even abundance can feel hollow.

More than the absence of conflict, inner peace is the presence of acceptance—the ability to rest in the present moment, at ease with oneself. It allows individuals to weather inevitable disappointments and setbacks without becoming embittered. When peace reigns within, circumstances lose their power to dictate one's state of mind.

In contrast, those who lack inner peace may find themselves consumed by comparison, envy, or regret, regardless of outward success. The euphoria of success and the pleasures associated with fame and fortune are often fleeting and temporary. The world's most celebrated figures have frequently spoken of the emptiness that can accompany fame or fortune—a testament to the irreplaceable value of inner tranquillity. Living life under constant public scrutiny and the pressure to conform to societal standards can lead to insecurities, anxiety, and a feeling of disconnect between one's public persona and true identity.

3.1 External Success is Fleeting

Achievements such as wealth, status, or career milestones are often temporary and subject to change. They can be lost, taken away, or become irrelevant over time. Once cultivated, inner peace is a lasting state of being. It is not dependent on external circumstances and can endure through life's ups and downs.

3.2 Inner Peace Brings True Fulfilment

While success can bring temporary satisfaction, it often leaves people feeling empty and drives them to chase the next goal. The pursuit of external validation can become a never-ending cycle. Peace within brings a deep sense of contentment and fulfilment. It allows you to appreciate the present moment and find joy in simply being, rather than constantly striving for more.

3.3 Inner Peace Aligns You with Your True Self

While external success can bring temporary rewards, inner peace offers a more profound and enduring sense of fulfilment, resilience, and well-being. It allows you to navigate life's challenges with grace, connect with your true self, and find contentment regardless of external circumstances. Ultimately, inner peace is the foundation for a meaningful and balanced life, one that surpasses the fleeting nature of external achievements.

4. A Lifelong Journey

Inner peace is not a destination reached overnight; it is a lifelong journey, shaped by practice, reflection, and growth. Different traditions offer varied paths—meditation, prayer, mindfulness, or acts of selfless service—but all lead towards the same destination: an unshakeable sense of well-being.

4.1 Awareness

The first step towards peace is noticing the patterns of one's own mind. Through honest self-reflection, individuals can become aware of the sources of their disquiet—fear, attachment, unresolved grief, or anger. This awareness is not meant to judge, but to illuminate.

4.2 Acceptance

Inner peace blossoms when one learns to accept both strengths and weaknesses, joys and sorrows, without resistance. Acceptance does not mean resignation; it is acknowledging reality without trying to force it into one's preferred shape. It is not about liking, wanting, or choosing, but about embracing what is.

4.3 Letting Go

Many of the mind's torments arise from clinging—clinging to expectations, outcomes, or past wounds. Letting go is the gentle art of releasing what no longer serves one's well-being, making room for new joys and insights.

American author and speaker Steve Maraboli (b. 1975) says, "*Letting go means to come to the realisation that some people are a part of your history, but not a part of your destiny.*"

4.4 Compassion

True peace cannot coexist with harsh self-judgement or resentment towards others. Cultivating compassion—for oneself and for all beings—softens the heart, allowing forgiveness and understanding to take root.

South African bishop and theologian, and 1984 Nobel Peace Prize winner Desmond Tutu (1931–2021) said, *"Compassion is not just feeling with someone, but seeking to change the situation. Frequently, people think compassion and love are merely sentimental. No! They are very demanding. If you are going to be compassionate, be prepared for action!"*

4.5 Presence

Inner peace lives in the present moment. Practices like mindfulness and meditation train the mind to rest in the present, rather than dwelling on the past or worrying about the future. In presence, one discovers that each moment, however ordinary, holds the potential for wonder.

Abraham Maslow declared, *"The ability to be in the present moment is a major component of mental wellness."*

5. The Gifts of Inner Peace

Those who have tasted inner peace describe it as the single most transformative experience of their lives. Far from dulling one's engagement with the world, tranquillity enhances it. When the storm inside abates, the beauty of simple things—sunlight through leaves, a child's laughter, the quiet hum of daily life—can be appreciated anew.

5.1 Resilience in Adversity

Inner peace acts as a buffer against the inevitable challenges life presents. Setbacks, losses, and uncertainties are met not with panic, but with calm resolve. This resilience does not ignore pain but allows it to be felt and processed without overwhelming despair. With peace as an anchor, life's waves may rock, but never capsize the soul.

In Maya Angelou's words, *"I can be changed by what happens to me. But I refuse to be reduced by it."*

Resilience is not simply bouncing back from adversity but adapting, growing, and using those experiences to shape a stronger, more capable self. It involves developing an unwavering belief in one's ability to overcome challenges and a commitment to keep moving forward despite the odds.

5.2 Deeper Relationships

When one is at peace with oneself, relationships with others flourish. The need to control, impress, or compete gives way to genuine connection and empathy. Peaceful individuals radiate warmth and acceptance, attracting trust and goodwill.

5.3 Creativity and Clarity

The mind at peace is not dulled; it is sharp, focused, and open to inspiration. Creativity flows more freely when not dammed by anxiety or self-doubt. Decisions are made with greater clarity, as one is less swayed by fear or impulse.

5.4 Freedom from Suffering

Perhaps the greatest gift of inner peace is liberation from needless suffering. While pain is an inevitable part of the human condition, much suffering is self-created, arising from resistance, rumination, or the expectation that life conform to one's desires. Peace offers freedom from these chains, allowing one to experience life as it is.

6. Inner Peace in the Modern World

In an era defined by speed, distraction, and information overload, the pursuit of inner peace can feel more elusive than ever. The modern world bombards us with constant stimuli—endless notifications, 24/7 news cycles, social media feeds, and the pressure to always be "on." This relentless pace can leave us feeling fragmented, anxious, and disconnected from ourselves. Yet, despite these challenges, the quest for inner peace remains not only relevant but essential.

6.1 Why Inner Peace Matters More Than Ever

The rise in anxiety, depression, and burnout is a direct consequence of our hyper-connected, fast-paced lives. Inner peace acts as a counterbalance, offering a sense of calm and stability in the face of external pressures.

Information overload can cloud our judgment and make it difficult to focus on what truly matters. Inner peace enables us to cut through the noise, allowing us to think clearly and make decisions that align with our values.

The modern world is marked by rapid change and unpredictability. Cultivating inner peace builds emotional resilience, enabling us to navigate uncertainty with greater ease and adaptability.

In a world of superficial interactions and digital distractions, inner peace enables us to form deeper, more meaningful connections with ourselves and others. It allows us to be fully present in our relationships.

6.2 Challenges to Inner Peace in the Modern Era

Smartphones and social media keep us tethered to the outside world, making it difficult to unplug and find moments of stillness.

There is a fear of missing out (FOMO). The pressure to keep up with trends, news, and social events can create a sense of urgency that disrupts our inner calm.

The sheer volume of information and stimuli we encounter daily can overwhelm our senses, leaving little room for reflection or introspection.

The expectation to excel in every aspect of life—career, relationships, health—can lead to stress and a sense of inadequacy.

6.3 How to Cultivate Inner Peace in a Fast-Paced World

Create tech-free zones or times in your day. For example, avoid checking your phone first thing in the morning or before bed. This helps create space for quiet reflection.

Slow down intentionally. Whether it's savouring a meal, taking a leisurely walk, or spending time in nature, slowing down allows us to reconnect with ourselves and the world around us.

Declutter your physical and mental space. Let go of unnecessary commitments, possessions, and distractions that drain your energy. Focus on what truly matters.

Be selective about the information you consume. Unfollow accounts or news sources that cause stress, and set limits on how much time you spend scrolling through social media.

6.4 The Paradox of Inner Peace in a Fast-Paced World

Ironically, the very things that make inner peace feel elusive—speed, distraction, and overload—are also the reasons why it is so vital. Inner peace is not about escaping the world; it is about finding a sense of calm and clarity within it. It is about creating a sanctuary within us that remains undisturbed, no matter how chaotic the external world becomes.

American musician John De Paola urged us to pause and let go of the frantic pace of life to find what truly matters. He says, *"Slow down and everything you are chasing will come around and catch you."*

While the challenges are real, the tools to cultivate inner peace are within our reach. By slowing down, setting boundaries, and prioritising mindfulness, we can reclaim our sense of calm and create a ripple effect of peace in our lives and the world around us. Inner peace is not the absence of chaos; it is the ability to remain centred in the midst of it. And in today's world, that ability is more valuable than ever.

7. The Ripple Effect of Inner Peace

The ripple effect is a powerful metaphor that illustrates how a single action or state of being can create waves of influence that extend far beyond its origin, much like the concentric circles formed when a pebble is dropped into still water. Inner peace functions in the same way—what begins as calm within an individual gradually radiates outward, shaping relationships, communities, and even societies.

When a person cultivates serenity, compassion, and mindfulness, others naturally respond to that energy. A peaceful presence can defuse tension, foster understanding, and inspire others to act with greater kindness and patience. In workplaces, it promotes collaboration and empathy; in families, it creates harmony and emotional stability. Over time, these subtle shifts accumulate, transforming collective consciousness.

The ripple effect reminds us that peace is not passive; it is an active force of change. Each choice—to listen instead of react, to forgive instead of resent—creates another ripple, touching unseen shores. As the Dalai Lama observed, "When you develop inner peace, you begin to feel the ripple effect—it affects your family, your community, and the whole world." Thus, the journey toward global peace begins not with governments or institutions, but within the quiet depths of the individual heart.

8. Summary

Inner peace is the ultimate experience because it allows every other experience—joy, sorrow, success, failure—to be met with openness and grace. In seeking peace, one does not turn away from the world but learns to embrace it fully, with all its beauty and imperfection. In nurturing this peace, we discover at last the truth that so many have sought across time and culture: that happiness is not something to be found, but something to be remembered, cultivated, and lived, moment by precious moment.

10
Spiritual Evolution

May there be peace in the heavens and sky,
peace on earth, peace in the waters,
peace in the plants, peace in the trees,
peace among the gods,
peace in Brahman (the ultimate reality),
peace everywhere. May that peace fill me.
Om Peace, Peace, Peace.

—Vedic Prayer

---

1. Peace As A Personal Quest

Peace is indeed fundamental, serving as a prerequisite for social and economic development, individual well-being, and the realisation of human rights, and is often considered a foundational element for a thriving society and a peaceful world. The right to peace is seen as a fundamental and essential human right, binding together the entire system of human rights and freedoms, as it is a prerequisite for the enjoyment of all other rights. Dr Kalam's assertion that "peace starts from within" means that inner peace is the foundation for external peace and harmony. That peace is cultivated internally rather than being found solely in external circumstances or possessions.

The quest for peace is a deeply personal and transformative journey that involves self-awareness, intentional living, and the cultivation of positive qualities. It is not about escaping from life's challenges but about finding tranquillity amidst them. By embarking on this quest, individuals can achieve a state of inner harmony that enhances their well-being, relationships, and overall quality of life. Peace, once attained, becomes a guiding light that illuminates the path of spiritual evolution and personal fulfilment.

The quest for inner peace has long been regarded as a private journey, an individual pursuit that brings solace and clarity to one's life. Yet, beneath the quiet surface of personal serenity lies a profound truth: the tranquillity cultivated within an individual does not remain confined but radiates outward, weaving through the lives of others and shaping the broader fabric of society. This phenomenon, often described as the "ripple effect" of inner peace, suggests that even the smallest pebble of calm dropped into the pond of human experience can create waves that reach distant and unexpected shores.

Inner peace is not the mere absence of turmoil, but a deep-rooted sense of contentment, balance, and acceptance. It is the harmonious alignment of thoughts, emotions, and actions, grounded firmly in self-awareness and compassion. This state can be cultivated through mindfulness, meditation, spiritual practice, creative expression, or simply being present in the moment. American psychiatrist and author Brian Weiss (b. 1944) writes, "Inner peace is impossible without patience. Wisdom requires patience. Spiritual growth implies the mastery of patience. Patience allows the unfolding of destiny to proceed at its own unhurried pace."

For some, inner peace is achieved through a process of letting go—releasing attachments, expectations, and resentments that cloud the mind and burden the heart. For others, it is found by embracing life's uncertainties and responding to them with equanimity. Regardless of the path taken, the tranquillity discovered within becomes a wellspring from which all other experiences flow. American author Robert Fulghum (b. 1937) says, "Peace is not something you wish for; it's something you make, something you do, something you are, and something you give away."

2. Honing Virtues

The transformation that inner peace brings to individuals stems from a deliberate and conscious effort to cultivate, refine, and perfect a particular moral or ethical quality within oneself. Honing virtues is a central aspect of spiritual evolution. Virtues are regarded as the foundational elements of a higher consciousness and a more moral, fulfilling life. As individuals cultivate virtues, they move closer to their true selves and to a state of unity with the divine or the universe. Virtues such as love, compassion, humility, and integrity are often seen as essential for achieving inner peace, harmony, and spiritual enlightenment. Virtue is described by Aristotle as a mean between two vices. Moral virtue lies in finding a balance, or "golden mean", between two extremes—one of excess and one of deficiency. For every virtue, there are two corresponding vices: one that represents excess (going too far) and one that represents deficiency (not going far enough). Virtue lies in avoiding both extremes and finding the mean that is appropriate to the situation. The "mean" is not a fixed or universal point, but rather it depends on the individual and the circumstances. What is virtuous in one situation may not be in another. For example, courage is a mean between recklessness (excess) and cowardice (deficiency), but the exact balance will vary depending on the context.

2.1 Examples of Virtues as Means Between Vices

Virtue	Deficiency (Vice)	Excess (Vice)
Courage	Cowardice	Recklessness
Generosity	Stinginess	Extravagance
Patience	Impatience	Passivity
Honesty	Deceitfulness	Brutal Honesty
Confidence	Timidity	Arrogance
Modesty	Shamelessness	Shyness
Temperance	Insensibility	Overindulgence

Extremes of behaviour—whether excessive or deficient—are often harmful to oneself and others. Virtue, as the mean, promotes harmony, balance, and well-being. Striving for the mean encourages self-awareness and self-improvement. It requires individuals to reflect on their actions and adjust their behaviour to achieve balance. The doctrine of the mean provides a framework for making ethical decisions. It encourages individuals to consider the context and find a balanced response rather than reacting impulsively or rigidly.

2.2 Human Flourishing (Eudaimonia)

Aristotle believed that living virtuously—finding the mean—is essential for eudaimonia, often translated as "flourishing" or "the good life". Virtue leads to a fulfilling and meaningful life. Unlike modern notions of happiness, which frequently focus on fleeting emotions or pleasure, eudaimonia refers to a deeper, more enduring state of well-being that arises from living a life of virtue, purpose, and fulfilment. Eudaimonia is not a temporary state but a long-term and enduring condition. It is the result of a lifetime of virtuous living and cannot be achieved through short-term pleasures or external rewards. Hungarian-American psychologist Mihaly Csikszentmihalyi (1934–2021) has drawn on Aristotle's ideas to develop theories of authentic happiness and flow, which emphasise the importance of meaning, purpose, and engagement in achieving a fulfilling life.

3. Transcendence

The influence of inner peace extends beyond the boundaries of the self. Like the gentle concentric circles created by a stone thrown into a lake, the qualities of calm, compassion, and understanding spread outward, touching the lives of friends, families, co-workers, and strangers alike.

3.1 Calm Contagion

Emotional states are inherently social. Science tells us that emotions are contagious; we absorb the moods and attitudes of those around us, often unconsciously. Calm contagion is the phenomenon where a quiet demeanour in one person can positively influence and reduce stress and anxiety in others. People can unconsciously mimic and absorb the emotional states of those around them through cues like body language, tone of voice, and facial expressions. In moments of heightened emotion, individuals, especially children, can "borrow" the nervous system of a calm, grounded person to help them return to a more balanced state. Someone who carries themselves with composure and equanimity can diffuse tension in a heated room, provide reassurance in moments of uncertainty, and inspire others to respond rather than react. When faced with conflict, a person-centred presence can de-escalate anger and invite dialogue, fostering environments where understanding prevails over discord.

3.2 How to avoid absorbing other people's emotions?

When you are in your personal space, try checking in with how you feel and tuning into your baseline. Awareness can help you distinguish between what belongs to you and what does not. Are you feeling more agitated, sad, or anxious? These may all be signs that you are picking up on someone else's energy. After social interactions, consider creating a ritual to help create some distance between you and what you might have absorbed. For example, you could take a shower after being in a crowded environment. You might also use your hands to "scoop" emotions out of your heart and push them away. Some may find smudging, called dhuman in Hindi, helpful. Sage (dhoop), which has a more pungent, herb-like scent, is known to clear all energies, both positive and negative, making it suitable for major energetic resets, such as after emotional events or when entering a new space. It has a stronger, herb-like aroma and is easier to keep lit, but is generally used to purify an area by dispersing smoke throughout. Sandalwood (incense sticks) is used to invite positive energy and promote relaxation, as well as mental clarity. Its scent is described as sweeter and fresher than sage, and although it can be more challenging to keep lit, it is excellent for daily cleansing or creating a peaceful environment.

4. Influencing Others

4.1 Role Modelling and Leadership

Leaders and influencers who demonstrate inner peace set a tone for those they guide. Their ability to remain composed under pressure, to make thoughtful decisions, and to respond to criticism with grace encourages others to emulate these traits. In workplaces, schools, and families, a peaceful presence can help resolve disputes, boost morale, and cultivate a culture of respect.

4.2 Communal and Societal Impact

The combined effect of many individuals seeking and sustaining inner peace can be transformative on a larger scale. As more people radiate calm and compassion, the collective atmosphere shifts. Communities become more resilient, inclusive, and harmonious.

4.3 Reducing Social Tension

When inner peace is widespread, it acts as a buffer against the stresses and divisions that often fracture society. Peaceful individuals are more likely to seek common ground, listen to differing perspectives, and work towards resolving conflicts. Over time, this shapes neighbourhoods, schools, and organisations into spaces where civility and cooperation are the norm, rather than the exception.

5. The Idea of Spiritual Evolution

The idea of spiritual evolution refers to the concept that the human soul or consciousness progresses through various stages of development over time, moving toward higher levels of awareness, wisdom, and unity with the divine or the universe. This concept is often rooted in spiritual, religious, and philosophical traditions, and it can be understood in different ways depending on the context. American philosopher, widely recognised as the father of American psychology, William James (1842–1910), said, "The greatest revolution of our generation is the discovery that human beings, by changing the inner attitudes of their minds, can change the outer aspects of their lives."

5.1 Progressive Growth

Spiritual evolution suggests that individuals (or humanity as a whole) are on a journey of inner growth. This growth involves moving from lower states of consciousness (such as fear, ego, and materialism) to higher states (such as love, compassion, and enlightenment). For example, in Hinduism, the soul (Atman) evolves through cycles of birth, death, and rebirth (samsara) until it achieves liberation (moksha). In Buddhism, the path to enlightenment involves progressing through stages of wisdom and compassion. Not only individuals, but humanity as a whole is also evolving spiritually. This collective evolution is seen as a movement toward greater unity, peace, and global consciousness.

5.2 Integration of Spirit and Matter

Spiritual evolution often involves integrating the spiritual and material aspects of life. It's not about rejecting the physical world but rather transcending its limitations while still engaging with it in a meaningful way. A central theme in spiritual evolution is the idea of reconnecting with a higher power, the divine, or the source of all existence. This can be understood as union with God (as in Christian mysticism), merging with the universe (as in pantheism), or realising one's true nature (as in Advaita Vedanta). Spiritual evolution emphasises inner transformation rather than external achievements. It involves cultivating virtues such as humility, gratitude, forgiveness, and unconditional love. Many spiritual traditions believe that the soul is eternal and that spiritual evolution occurs over multiple lifetimes. This idea is central to reincarnation beliefs in Hinduism, Buddhism, and other Eastern philosophies.

5.3 A New Divider

In contemporary spirituality, the concept of spiritual evolution is often associated with personal growth, mindfulness, and the pursuit of meaning. It is viewed as a means to navigate the challenges of modern life by cultivating inner peace, purpose, and a connection to something greater than oneself. Some critics argue that the concept of spiritual evolution can lead to a sense of superiority among those who believe they are "more evolved" than others. Since spiritual evolution is essentially a metaphysical concept, it isn't easy to measure or prove scientifically. The idea of spiritual evolution can sometimes be influenced by cultural or religious biases, leading to a narrow understanding of what constitutes "higher" or "lower" states of consciousness.

The idea of spiritual evolution offers a framework for understanding the human journey as one of growth, transformation, and transcendence. Whether viewed through the lens of ancient traditions or modern spirituality, it encourages individuals to seek deeper meaning, cultivate virtues, and strive for unity with the divine or the cosmos. While it is a deeply personal and subjective concept, it continues to inspire people across cultures and generations.

6. Peace is the Ultimate Destination of Spiritual Evolution

The highest goal of spiritual growth is to attain a state of inner and outer peace. Spiritual evolution often involves self-awareness, mindfulness, and the cultivation of inner tranquillity. Practices such as meditation, prayer, and introspection help individuals release negative emotions, attachments, and ego-driven desires, leading to a state of inner calm and contentment.

Many spiritual paths teach that true peace comes from aligning oneself with the natural flow of life or the cosmos. This involves accepting the impermanence of things, embracing compassion, and living in harmony with others and the environment. Spiritual evolution often involves moving beyond dualistic thinking (good vs. evil, self vs. other) to a more unified understanding of existence. This shift in perspective can dissolve conflict and foster a sense of oneness, leading to profound peace. Peace is not just an individual pursuit but also a collective one. By serving others and cultivating compassion, individuals contribute to a more peaceful world, which in turn reinforces their spiritual growth.

In some traditions, such as Hinduism or Buddhism, the ultimate goal of spiritual evolution is liberation (moksha or nirvana) from the cycle of suffering and rebirth. This liberation is often described as a state of eternal peace and bliss. While Moksha and Nirvana both represent the ultimate goal of spiritual liberation, they differ in their philosophical underpinnings, particularly in their views on the self and the nature of liberation. Moksha emphasises the unity of the individual soul with the universal reality, while Nirvana focuses on the cessation of suffering and the realisation of no-self.

In essence, the journey of spiritual evolution is viewed as a path toward transcending the turbulence of the human experience and attaining a state of profound inner peace, as well as a deeper understanding of the world. This peace is not just the absence of conflict but a deep, abiding sense of wholeness, connection, and fulfilment.

7. Practical Steps Towards Inner Peace

Recognising the ripple effect of inner peace invites a commitment to its cultivation. While the journey is deeply personal, there are universal practices that can support it:

7.1 Mindfulness and Meditation

Regular mindfulness practice grounds individuals in the present and helps quieten the mind's chatter, fostering deeper awareness and acceptance. According to British and American writer and speaker Alan Watts (1915–1973), "Meditation is the discovery that the point of life is always arrived at in the immediate moment." Most of the time, the only thing standing between you and peace is your brain. Practise quietening the mind to find inner calm while acknowledging the universal struggle of overthinking.

7.2 Self-Compassion

Self-compassion is the practice of treating yourself with the same kindness, understanding, and care that you would offer to a close friend, especially during times of failure, difficulty, or personal suffering. It involves recognising that imperfection, pain, and struggle are part of the shared human experience, and responding to your shortcomings with warmth and patience rather than harsh criticism or judgement. Self-compassion involves being gentle and understanding with yourself rather than being overly critical or harsh when you make mistakes or face challenges.

7.3 Gratitude Journaling

Reflecting daily on things to be grateful for can shift one's focus from a state of lack to one of abundance, nurturing a peaceful mindset. According to spiritual leader Sri Chinmoy (1931–2007), "Gratitude is the sweetest thing in a seeker's life—in all human life. If there is gratitude in your heart, then there will be tremendous sweetness in your eyes."

7.4 Nature Immersion

Time spent in natural surroundings has been shown to soothe the nervous system and inspire a sense of connection. According to Scottish-born American naturalist John Muir (1838–1914), "Nature is always lovely, invincible, glad, whatever is done and suffered by her creatures. All scars she heals, whether in rocks or water or sky or hearts. The clearest way into the Universe is through a forest wilderness. In every walk with nature, one receives far more than he seeks."

7.5 Community Engagement

Building supportive relationships and contributing to causes larger than oneself enhances feelings of belonging and purpose. Mahatma Gandhi said, "The best way to find yourself is to lose yourself in the service of others." Engagement is the key to success in any community. It's not just about showing up; it's about being present and involved. Nineteenth-century American Confederate States Army general and author Albert Pike (1809–1891) said it so aptly, "What we do for ourselves dies with us. What we do for others and the world remains and is immortal."

8. Sat-Chit-Ananda

Sat-Chit-Ananda, also known as Sacchidananda in Sanskrit, is a profound concept in Hindu philosophy and spirituality, particularly in Advaita Vedanta and Kashmir Shaivism. It is often translated as "Existence-Consciousness-Bliss" and represents the essential nature of the ultimate reality, Brahman, or the Self (Atman). It is a profound concept that encourages individuals to delve into the depths of their being, recognise their inherent connection with the divine, and experience the ultimate reality as truth, consciousness, and bliss.

8.1 Sat

Sat refers to the eternal, unchanging reality that underlies all existence. It is the fundamental essence of being, which is always present and never ceases to exist. In this context, Brahman is described as the ultimate truth, the source of all that exists.

8.2 Chit

Chit represents the pure, self-aware consciousness that is the basis of all perception, thought, and knowledge. It is the knowing principle that illuminates the mind and the world. In the state of enlightenment, one realises that this consciousness is not limited to the individual but is universal and identical with Brahman.

8.3 Ananda

Ananda signifies the infinite, unconditional bliss that is the natural state of the Self when it is free from ignorance, desire, and suffering. It is not a temporary emotional state but an eternal, unshakeable joy that arises from the realisation of one's true nature as Brahman.

Sat-Chit-Ananda provides a practical framework for a balanced and meaningful life by encouraging individuals to seek truth, cultivate consciousness through mindfulness and introspection, and act with righteousness. Harmony between truth and awareness is believed to lead to lasting fulfilment. To realise one's true nature as Sat-Chit-Ananda leads to liberation (moksha) from the cycle of birth and death (samsara).

9. Summary

When individuals cultivate their sense of calm, acceptance, and contentment, they are better equipped to extend that peace to their relationships and the world at large. Inner peace, though deeply personal, is far from a self-contained achievement. Its influence radiates outward, subtly shaping the interactions, relationships, and environments we inhabit. As more people embark on this inward journey, the cumulative waves have the power to transform not only individual lives but the very foundation of communities and, ultimately, our shared humanity.

10. Conclusion

Let us therefore recognise the significance of seeking inner peace—not merely for ourselves, but for the world that is quietly and inexorably shaped by the ripples we send into its waters through personal effort.

About the Author

Arun Tiwari is a distinguished Indian missile scientist, engineer, professor, and author whose career spans both the frontiers of defence technology and the landscape of inspirational literature. He is best known worldwide as the close associate and co-author of Dr A.P.J. Abdul Kalam, the former President of India, on the iconic autobiography *Wings of Fire*. Tiwari's life embodies a rare confluence: the rigour of scientific innovation, the art of storytelling, and a commitment to using knowledge for human upliftment.

Born in 1955 in Meerut, he graduated with a master's degree in mechanical engineering from GB Pant University. He joined the Defence Research and Development Organisation (DRDO) in 1982, working under Dr Kalam in the Integrated Guided Missile Development Programme (IGMDP). Over the next two decades, he played a pivotal role in creating indigenous hardware systems for the Trishul and Akash surface-to-air missiles, particularly in the development of advanced aluminium alloys and titanium technologies. His work established him as a key contributor to India's quest for self-reliance in strategic defence.

But Tiwari's legacy extends far beyond the laboratory. His career is marked by a belief that technology must ultimately serve society. In the mid-1990s, he collaborated with renowned cardiologist Dr B. Soma Raju to develop the country's first low-cost coronary implant—the Kalam-Raju Stent—an achievement that earned him the prestigious Defence Technology Spin-Off Award. Later, he pioneered telemedicine applications and helped shape the initial phase of the Pan-Africa e-Network, bringing the benefits of broadband connectivity to remote healthcare.

Alongside his technical contributions, Tiwari has built an extraordinary literary body of work. Beyond *Wings of Fire*, his books explore the intersections of science, spirituality, leadership, and social change. He has also published the essence of the great Indian scriptures in English, making timeless wisdom accessible to contemporary readers worldwide. His writings often return to a central theme: that behind all technology, knowledge, and creativity lies the enigma of manifestation—the real intelligence of the cosmos—which works silently through human beings and reveals itself in flashes of discovery, compassion, and service.

His voice reaches further through his digital presence: since 019, his fortnightly blog (aruntiwari.com) has been widely read, ering reflections on current events, innovation, and philosophy. ough these writings, he has come to be regarded as a "spiritual nalist"—a thinker who balances mysticism with scientific . Teaching at the University of Hyderabad for a decade as unct Professor at the School of Management Studies, he ed a renowned course on Medical Humanities for MBA

As a teacher, speaker, and author, Arun Tiwari continues to bridge the worlds of technology and human aspiration. His journey—from missiles to medicine, scriptures to cyberspace—underscores a singular truth: that the greatest intelligence is not what we create, but what is revealed through us, in the quiet miracle of manifestation itself.

Books by Arun Tiwari

Published by Sakal Publications

- The Baton Should Not Fall
- Decoding the Pandemic
- India Wakes : Post Coronavirus New World Order
- Innovate Locally to Win Globally
- Live for a Legacy
- Uddhava Gita
- Discovery of Anugita
- Simple Spirituality : Recalling Kabir
- A Modern Interpretation of Tulsidas Ramcharitramanas
- A Modern Interpretation of Lokmanya Tilak's Gita Rahasya
- We are What We Eat
- Yoga Vasishtha
- Spectrum
- Neo-ethical Living